BUDO
MIND
AND
BODY

Budo Mind and Body

◆◆◆

Training Secrets *of the* Japanese Martial Arts

◆◆◆

Nicklaus Suino

Weatherhill
Boston & London   2007

Weatherhill
An imprint of Shambhala Publications, Inc.
Horticultural Hall
300 Massachusetts Avenue
Boston, Massachusetts 02115
www.shambhala.com

This is a revised and updated edition of a book previously published in 1996 under the title *Arts of Strength, Arts of Serenity.*

The techniques of the martial arts are dangerous if not practiced correctly. Neither the author nor the publisher is responsible for the results of your choice to practice these techniques; you do so at your own risk. Please use caution when handling any weapons and be sure to consult a qualified teacher before attempting to perform any new martial arts skills.

9 8 7 6 5 4 3 2 1

First Paperback Edition
Printed in the United States of America

⊛ This edition is printed on acid-free paper that meets the American National Standards Institute z39.48 Standard. Distributed in the United States by Random House, Inc., and in Canada by Random House of Canada Ltd

Interior design and composition: Greta D. Sibley & Associates

The Library of Congress catalogues the previous edition of this book as follows:
Suino, Nicklaus.
Budo mind and body: training secrets of the Japanese martial arts / Nicklaus Suino.—1st ed.
p. cm.
Rev. ed. of: Arts of strength, arts of serenity. 1996.
Includes bibliographical references.
ISBN 978-0-8348-0568-2 (hardcover)
ISBN 978-0-8348-0573-6 (paperback)
1. Martial arts—Japan—Training. 2. Martial arts—Japan—Psychological aspects.
I. Suino, Nicklaus. Arts of strength, arts of serenity. II. Title.
GV1100.77.A2S85 2006
613.7'148—dc22
2005042353

*To Pamela
Enchanting,
Enlightened,
Light of my life*

CONTENTS

PREFACE

THE MATERIAL in this book was first published in 1996, with the title *Arts of Strength, Arts of Serenity*. In the years since, it has been my distinct pleasure to have feedback from many readers, both newcomers to budo and accomplished martial artists. I am happy to say that most readers were kind—graciously pointing out sections of the book they enjoyed—and that only a few chose to point out the areas where I could have done better. Except for one or two copies on my martial arts bookshelf, the first edition completely sold out.

Some superb instructors have honored me by recommending this book to their martial arts students. Paul Godshaw, of Mission Viejo, California, who runs a brilliant Shotokan karate dojo, has a few copies that he hands out to his students when it seems appropriate. Gary Legacy, of St. Thomas, Ontario, who heads up a huge organization of expert Shorin-ryu karate students, recognized our kindred goals in teaching budo and brought a few of his black-belts along to our iaido practice sessions. John Gage, of Tokyo, Japan, head of the foreign department of the International Martial Arts Federation (IMAF), has done more to support my martial arts adventures than any other human being.

Further, I am happy to say that my Japanese mentors, Yamaguchi Katsuo Sensei and Sato Shizuya Sensei, have not yet disowned me for the words written here. My personal view is that the explanations in this book are as timely as ever.

Training in traditional martial arts is one of the most valuable pursuits I know, and the admonitions in these pages to train with intensity and work tirelessly for self-improvement still ring true. The evolution of budo continues. Some products of change are good—great technicians are refining their techniques to make them more effective than ever—and some are dubious. More than ever, charlatans are offering martial arts instruction with no historical basis or practical effectiveness. I hope this book will guide students away from these schools and towards instructors who practice the philosophy set forth in these pages.

So it was with no small pleasure that I agreed to revise this material for publication when asked to do so by Beth Frankl, gracious martial arts editor at Shambhala, herself an accomplished student of aikido. Some sections have been rearranged to emphasize the real mission of this book; to point out that budo is an endeavor with a distinct goal involving the body, mind, and spirit. Many small editorial changes have been made. The resources sections in the appendix have been updated. We have worked hard to eliminate any errors of fact or form.

I hope this book is a benefit to you, the reader, as you explore the world of budo. It is a lifelong quest with many challenges, and still more rewards. I congratulate you for stepping onto the path to enlightenment.

B U D O

M I N D

A N D

B O D Y

A man who has mastered an art reveals it in his every action.
—Samurai maxim

AFTER A HARD DAY of martial arts practice, while enjoying a cold drink with training partners, we sometimes share stories of the masters of old. These are stories of men and women who were able to perform feats of martial skill that seem almost magical to us today. The stories are an inspiration to train harder, and they hint at what might be possible if we keep practicing long enough. The images are so compelling that whole systems of study have grown up around certain masters—men like Ueshiba Morihei, the founder of aikido, who was said to be able to throw his students to the ground with the strength of a single finger. Ueshiba could casually drop two, three, or even ten attackers. At the same time, there was more to the old master than mere physical skill. Considered an enlightened man,

Ueshiba was known for such sayings as "Love is the highest principle of the martial arts," and "To injure an opponent is to injure yourself."

According to the stories, there was always something about these masters that resonated beyond their great skill. Mifune Kyuzo, perhaps the greatest technician ever to come out of the Kodokan (the original judo institution), was known for the softness of his techniques. He was able to defeat students twice his size while barely seeming to expend any effort. People who trained with him later said, "It was like fighting with an empty jacket." Mifune was a great historian of the martial arts, and developed theories of physical interaction that are still studied by judoists.

There have been swordsmen in Japan's samurai history who reached a point in their training where they were able to say, "I cannot be defeated by anyone in the world." The legendary Miyamoto Musashi and Yamaoka Tesshu each reportedly made this claim—in different eras, of course—and nobody was ever able to prove them wrong. The swordsmen who faced these men would be unable to detect any opening for an attack. Both men were great artists with a brush, and Yamaoka was a preeminent statesman.

A similar story is told about a martial artist named Matsumura Sokon, one of the pioneers of Okinawan karate.

A skilled opponent, determined to fight him, tried three times to mount an attack, but each time was driven back by the sheer physical energy emanating from Matsumura. The actual physical battle never took place because Matsumura's challenger was unable to gather himself to strike.

It would be easy to dismiss these stories as legends, exaggerated by the admiration of students for their teachers and by the passage of time, had I not witnessed similar feats by living martial arts masters. These were not the kind of tricks you see when you watch a martial arts movie; any well-motivated and talented athlete could learn the spinning kicks and flips you see on film. The feats I saw were impressive not so much as physical skills—although such skills do require years of practice to master—but as reflections of inner strength. One living example of such a modern master is Sato Shizuya, a judo and jujutsu teacher. Like his own teacher, Mifune Kyuzo, Mr. Sato has an uncanny ability to throw his students around the mat like rag dolls. Further, when he does it, he is relaxed, apparently thinking about something else. I know that he hardly uses any physical strength because he used to toss me around when I trained with him in Japan over fourteen years ago. I was thirty years old at the time, and he was around sixty-two.

I continue to view him as a source of great energy and wisdom.

Another one of my teachers, Yamaguchi Katsuo, is a swordsman known around the world. He underwent treatment for stomach cancer in 1993, and is very elderly now, but between 1988 and 1992, watching him perform formal exercises with the sword was an almost religious experience. At sword demonstrations in Japan, hundreds of swordsmen and women will perform in groups of four or five at a time. The audience often loses interest after an hour or two, even when watching some of the most famous swordsmen in the country. When Yamaguchi-Sensei performed, however, everyone was rapt. A calm would fall over the audience and the air would become charged with a feeling of reverence. At a special event held at the American Embassy dojo (martial arts hall) in Tokyo, a group of twenty-five or thirty North American kids had a chance to see Yamaguchi-Sensei perform. These kids were holy terrors; we worked hard to keep them busy and to tire them out during their one-hour judo lesson each week, but they were never quiet and never still. You can guess who was more exhausted at the end of each class! Even this rambunctious group, however, fell silent when the old master began to swing his sword. They were absolutely entranced for the entire fifteen minutes of his demonstration. The only sound they made was an occasional gasp when his sword whooshed through the air.

The physical ability of all these men is indeed impressive, but they also have a kind of calm strength which some would say has a spiritual source. Indeed, many of these men would themselves say that the source of their unique skills is in the spiritual realm, and an important part of Japanese martial arts philosophy is that students learn to let nature, or "spirit," generate their techniques. Even if you don't believe in such concepts, you can watch the masters and see that they are extraordinarily focused, their movements are very efficient, and that they radiate a quiet inner strength. They express martial spirit in every motion—real martial spirit, not the kind you pay to see in the movies.

How do they get to be so exceptional? This question has fascinated martial arts students in the West ever since students started returning from Japan with incredible stories of their teachers and the legendary masters. Asian martial arts have flourished in the West in the past sixty years, yet there are very few Western teachers who merit the title "master" in the same way as do the elder teachers I met in

Japan. There are some crucial elements in the training and culture of the Japanese masters not easily transplanted to foreign soil. I found that the people who so impressed me with their serenity and wisdom had practiced one of the traditional art forms of Japan for at least of couple of decades. Besides the martial arts, some of the well-known traditional arts are tea ceremony, calligraphy, and playing classical musical instruments (such as the *shakuhachi*, or bamboo flute). Many also practice Zen.

When I lived in Japan, I saw so many people improving themselves through different types of traditional activities that I began to want to know more about the characteristics shared by all these arts, particularly the different forms of *budo* (the general Japanese term for martial arts). I thought it might be possible to extract these characteristics and make them available to those who wanted to become better martial artists. In fact, after nearly four decades of practice, I have learned that most of what once seemed mysterious or esoteric about budo is actually fairly simple and practical. My teachers have shown me that the principles of one martial art are usually found in the others as well.

All this suggests that the principles underlying these different arts are common to an even wider variety of physical arts, but since I am no expert in tea ceremony or traditional brush painting, the descriptions and explanations in this book will center on martial arts. Thoughtful readers could apply them to other areas of life, however, and I encourage them to do so.

The real secret to becoming an expert in martial arts is realizing that training is a process of self-discovery. Further, it is a means of modifying your personality to make yourself healthier, more well balanced, and more efficient. Outside of Japan, this idea has for the most part been lost, and the budo forms are typically taught as nothing more than specialized fighting methods. This approach is wasteful, however, for in the short term, there are much more efficient ways to teach fighting than the highly ritualized practice of traditional martial arts. Only when an art is considered as a whole system, including its "internal" aspects, can all the cultural content be justified. Ironically, taking this larger view, the "excess baggage" of ritual and spiritual components in these arts makes them better, more efficient tools for personal cultivation even while complicating the process of learning how to fight.

This apparent contradiction is not as troublesome a problem for serious students of budo as it would seem, since there is not much real need for most of us to learn how to fight. The study of budo forms, which were codified during a time in Japan's history when there was an emphasis on martial arts study for self-cultivation, is ideally suited for people wanting to develop a deep inner calm and confidence. Certainly in contemporary society, we have a much greater need for calm wisdom than for efficient killing skills. This doesn't mean that everybody who reads this book and tries to follow all the advice found in it is going to become a great master or guru. To become really great at something requires luck and talent, as well as the same long years of practice that everybody must put in to become merely good. Following my suggestions for learning a martial art should help you become better at it. You will become more efficient at your chosen art, and hopefully get more enjoyment out of it. If you keep at it long enough, you should find that other areas of your life are improving, too.

If you want to go further, however, if the spiritual and philosophical accomplishments of the people I have described appeal to you, then you will have to give serious thought to the deeper issues that are raised here, and probably do a lot of other research as well. As I advise in later chapters, students who want to become great martial artists must read everything they can get their hands on, train fanatically for an extended period of time, and reflect deeply on the relationship between budo training and their lives.

Some material that relates to the inner aspects of budo will be too esoteric for a few readers. I have tried to present it in a straightforward manner, without too much religious or spiritual content, for those who think such issues less important. It is, however, well worth anyone's time to give serious thought to those matters as well as the practical matters inherent in martial arts training.

Real budo mastery is not for everyone. The path is too hard for most people, and some of the rewards are less than obvious. Traditional martial artists do not make a lot of money, and there is little recognition of great budo practitioners, even in Japan. Most who idolize martial arts teachers are needy people who require a great deal of attention themselves.

If you want to find a path with heart, however, and are sure that money and praise are not too important to you, budo may be the right place to look. Even those who practice budo as a hobby will realize many of its benefits. The rewards—better health, increased confidence, calmness, and insight—are evident even in the short term. The benefits of a lifetime of practice are deeper than those more material rewards that come from common pursuits.

Once you start making progress along the martial arts path, you will find that the things you learn allow you to prosper in your work, your hobbies, and in relationships. You will find that your ability to handle a crisis improves, and that your satisfaction with life increases. These improvements can be brought about if you immerse yourself in the study of real budo and commit yourself fully to the ideas found in it. The triumph that you may have thought would come through defeating others, you will find comes instead from learning to love the training itself, and from living honestly, without self-delusion, in the real world.

The person to whom this book is most likely to appeal is one who believes that, in some way, he or she could be a little closer—physically, mentally, or spiritually—to what he or she ideally wants to be. Such a person must believe that improvement is possible, and that success, in some form, is worth striving for. He or she must believe in something larger or more important than him- or herself, such as the dojo, family, God, or country; be willing to work to benefit that larger concept; and take satisfaction from doing that work every day.

The bottom line is that almost everybody wants to make his or her life better in some way, and this book is both a practical guide to one way of accomplishing this and an exhortation to undertake the task with as much commitment as possible. Budo is a pursuit that provides infinite opportunities for growth; it gives back as much as you put into it. Even if you don't have five hours a day or a lifetime to devote to practice, you can enjoy training and reap some of its benefits. The simple key to realizing those benefits is throwing yourself into practice with great enthusiasm.

1

Training the Body

The Way is in training.
—Miyamoto Musashi

Physical Training

The foundation of martial arts, that which gives them their unique character, is built on physical training. This may make the arts seem primitive, in the same way we think of ancient dance rituals as primitive, but it also grounds them in the real world. There is no avoiding the toil and sweat required to learn martial arts skills, and you should be suspicious of anyone who promises results without long, hard work.

The work is, in fact, the very thing that makes budo worthwhile, because almost everything good that comes from budo comes from the process of physically training the body over a long period of time. The health benefits, such as improved circulation, stamina, and strength, come from repetitive motions of the body itself, starting with lighter, less strenuous motions and building up to more taxing drills as we advance. Mental benefits are the result of seeing hard work pay off in the form of improved skill. We learn that our efforts produce results, and, if we have good teachers, we learn to generalize the concept of discipline and apply it to all sorts of activities, not just budo. The so-called spiritual rewards of training, such as a sense of well-being, of place in society, and of purpose in life, come in large part from the feeling of hard work well done that we get at the end of the training day.

Experience tells us that there are better and worse ways to work, however. One lifetime is barely enough to master a single martial art, much less the several arts that many people practice these days, and there are always distractions from training. The road to mastery is so long that we must learn to be as efficient as possible as we travel it. Many great people have studied the learning process and have added refinements to the way we practice. Some have made mistakes that we can try to avoid. We can benefit from their experiences by understanding history and the principles of learning, greatly improving our chances of following a smooth path as we progress.

What follows is a discussion of six selected aspects of physical training that almost four decades of martial art study have led me to believe are particularly important.

Progressive Skill Development

Progressive skill development is a vital key to long-term progress in budo. The Japanese were the first to start granting belt ranks, reflecting the many advancements they made in systematizing the learning process. This was one of their most important contributions to the development of martial arts.

Instead of randomly presenting material and hoping that students would catch on, the Japanese formalized the process of introducing basic material to beginning students, and gradually increasing the complexity and difficulty of the material as students became more advanced. Principles that were learned at the beginning would become reflexive through long practice. Later, the instructor could concentrate on teaching more advanced concepts, knowing that students would already be able to hold a strong stance, for example, or be able to throw a punch without any glaring weaknesses.

Failure to take this incremental and progressive approach can limit one's potential for long-term growth. Many students who start training in competitive martial arts, or who learn in a casual environment (from a friend, for example), reach a certain level of competence and never progress beyond it. If they are naturally talented, or very dedicated and hard working, they can become fairly skilled, usually reaching their peak in two to three years, but problems can occur that limit their growth after the initial training period.

One problem is that they have no tools for teaching themselves to get better. They learned by being exposed to a technique, practicing it a little, then trying it out in the ring. In this context, students learn to think of techniques in terms of those that work and those that do not, rather than as more and less advanced skills. Powerfully effective techniques that may take hours to master are ignored, because they do not yield any benefits when first tried.

Progressive skill development, on the other hand, allows you to practice lesser, simpler skills first, gaining ability and confidence in those skills before going on to others that may be more difficult. The period in which you learn these skills also gives your teacher a chance to closely examine your basic skills, and to make sure that you have no serious weaknesses that might cause you trouble later. You can prosper in your martial arts training by adopting a progressive approach.

Always concentrate on the simpler things first. Everyone learns to crawl before learning to walk, and you cannot expect to perform an advanced karate kata unless you know how to stand in a strong, well-balanced front stance. In karate, iaido, and kyudo, spend time making sure that your stances are good, because everything else depends on them. In judo, jujutsu, aikido, and kendo, be sure that you understand how to move in a balanced manner. If you do not develop an intuitive understanding of balance, you will never be good at these arts.

The progression of kata taught in arts such as karate is also designed to teach skills in a progressive manner. You learn certain kata first because they are simpler, and because the connections between one move and the next involve less difficult transitions. Take the time to master the kata you are being taught now before growing impatient to learn a new one. Most of the students I have seen who are constantly requesting new material are not very good at the material they have already been taught. This shows clearly that they do not understand everything about the early forms. Any more kata piled on top of the first will simply reveal the same fundamental weaknesses.

Break It Down

When learning a new technique, try it first in its entirety. Chances are that you will have some difficulty performing it with confidence. Instead of repeating the whole technique over and over, determine the parts at which you are weakest, and practice them separately. If there are even smaller parts of those portions that still give you trouble, isolate those and practice them. This is what is meant by "break it down." Once you have achieved a reasonable degree of mastery over each part, you can then put them back together into one complete technique.

To take a very simple example, consider a two-handed aikido technique such as *tenchi-nage* ("heaven and earth throw"). This throw is a counter to an attack in which the opponent grabs both your wrists. In it, you step forward, passing the opponent on his right side while leading him down with your left hand (earth) and reaching over him in front with your right (heaven). If the opponent does not fall smoothly to the ground, there must be some weakness in your execution.

Break the movement down by practicing the heaven hand and earth hand separately. While doing so, look carefully at each part of the movement to see that it is doing what it should. If stepping and moving the earth hand at the same time does not give good results, practice the step and the hand movements separately. Keep breaking down and refining the parts of a technique until you can perform it with strength, and in a fluid and balanced manner.

Determine the Principle

Always look for the principle that makes a technique work. If you can determine what the principle is, then you will be able to learn the technique better and will also eventually discover other techniques that operate on the same principle. Subjecting each new technique to such intense mental scrutiny is more difficult than simply doing what you are told, but undertaking it is what separates the serious martial artist from the hobbyist.

There are no skills in the martial arts that exist without a foundation. Every technique is based on a larger or deeper principle that can be applied to other techniques. Punching relies on using the largest muscle groups in the upper body in a coordinated manner to achieve the strongest extension of the arm. Stances depend on correct bone alignment to direct power from the ground through to the body and the limbs. Many throws are based on the idea of using a figurative lever and fulcrum to upset an opponent's balance. If you understand the notion that putting your hips lower than your opponent's hips gives you an advantage in power when throwing, then you can strive to lower your hips in every forward throw, and thereby overcome one of the major obstacles to performing such techniques well.

As another example, consider the structure of the human hand. When that hand grabs your wrist, its weakest point is the space between the thumb and forefinger. When attempting to escape from that grab, it makes the most sense to apply pressure to the area where there is space, not muscle and bone. In one common escape technique found in jujutsu, we pivot the forearm so that the leverage is applied against the thumb and fingers, and the attacker's hand naturally opens just enough to allow the forearm to slip out.

Once you understand and apply this principle, locating the weakest point in the attack and concentrating your energy there, you will find that all your escape techniques work better.

Repetition

Many students come into the dojo thinking that there is some magic trick to learning the martial arts. They imagine that if the instructor would simply reveal the secret to them, all their difficulties would vanish. Common sense tells us that this is not so; if it were, there would be far more masters than students. The "magic" in martial arts is simply the teaching power of repetition. It is possible to walk into a dojo as a nervous, clumsy student and walk out as a confident, skilled instructor, but the transformation takes years, and only occurs if the student throws him- or herself into the training body and soul.

Repetition is the magic that makes us both strong and physically capable of performing a technique. This is true in any physical endeavor, and especially true in the martial arts. Repetition is also the magic that gives us our understanding of the principles that underlie the techniques.

Constant practice forces us to compare many different types of techniques, physically if not mentally, and to draw conclusions about how and when they work best. This action, done often enough and over a long enough period of time, leads students to the intuitive grasp of principles that is the foundation for real progress in budo. Repetition is the key to the peculiar mental state sought by Zen practitioners and martial artists called "no-mind," which we will discuss in greater detail in a later chapter. Almost nothing in the martial arts is possible without repetition.

Conditioning the Body

I am always surprised when I meet someone who claims to be a martial artist or martial arts instructor, but who is obviously out of shape. An instructor who cannot train for an entire class alongside his students is unlikely to be much of an instructor at all. Only extreme old age or recent injury are acceptable excuses for standing on the sidelines barking orders. Nearly all of the master instructors I met in Japan were not only of higher rank than their students, but were clearly better at performing the techniques of their art. Those who could not perform as well were almost all over seventy years of age.

Martial arts are physical. I emphasize this again here because there are so many budoists out there who exercise the muscles of the jaw more regularly than any others. Sincere physical commitment is the key to healthy martial arts training over the long term, and almost no student has ever become really expert without an extended period of intense exercise that approached the limits of his or her physical endurance. Through hard training, physical skills become mental certainties, and mental certainties lead to a calm spirit. The more thoroughly the physical components are practiced and cultivated, the more clearly the other aspects will be revealed.

This physical training can take many forms. The most obvious are the different repetitive conditioning drills. In striking arts, punching hundreds or thousands of times with power is very beneficial. Striking a *makiwara* (a device used for conditioning the hands, arms, feet, and legs, usually a thick board wrapped in leather or rope) for long periods of time is a traditional means of training the body.

In judo, an exercise called *uchi-komi* is used. Two training partners grasp each other in the usual judo fashion, then one executes a throwing technique up to the point just before the actual throw. He or she repeats the drill ten times or so, then the other partner performs an equal number of repetitions. The more sets, the better the results. As long as both partners have built up their bodies through training to be able to endure the high numbers, there is no reason not to do a few hundred of these uchi-komi in each training session.

While I was living in Japan, my training partner and I undertook to complete ten thousand uchi-komi of our favorite techniques. We only had time to train together on Saturdays, so it took a few months to reach our goal. During the training, we learned a great deal about these techniques, and though the number itself doesn't mean we reached perfection, I recall that the techniques worked very well in competition, and that we both felt very satisfied on the day we reached ten thousand. I recommend this approach to anybody serious about judo training.

In iaido, train by making many thousands of sword cuts. In kyudo, train by shooting arrows until you are exhausted. In kendo, strike the opponent until you cannot lift your *shinai* even one more time. In aikido, resolve to throw and be thrown until you cannot get up. Although not many students will have the heart to follow it to the end, this is the way to success.

Purification

An important concept in budo is that of self-purification through training. Budo practice is thought by some to be a means of approaching the presence of the sacred. In some ways similar to the ritual of washing the hands and mouth before entering a temple, training is a way of cleansing the body, mind, and spirit in preparation for an encounter with a higher plane of existence.

The physical cleansing that takes place is fairly obvious. Sweat cleans out the pores, and the rush of blood through the veins and arteries is thought to help keep them clear. Comparing the physical condition of a budo-man at seventy years of age, and that of someone the same age who has not trained, will satisfy you that exercise is good for the body. If, in fact, "the body is a temple," then hard physical training is equivalent to sweeping the floors of the temple, painting the walls, and burning incense to welcome the gods.

Mental cleansing comes through concentration. The complex actions performed in budo require our strict attention, distracting us from petty concerns. Paradoxically, deep concentration on the details of technique frees us from worrying about daily issues, allowing us to concentrate on more fundamental matters. Thus, we can look clearly at our circumstances and decide if they are what we think they ought to be. In a lesser sense, this can mean something like examining a technique and deciding the best way to perform it. In a larger sense, it can mean contemplating our whole relationship with the world, and perhaps making behavioral changes that bring us more in line with our ideas of how we ought to live.

Through frequent practice, we learn to stay in this state of sharpened perception for longer periods of time. Repeated efforts of this kind eventually sharpen perception permanently. Like the results of regular meditation, daily exposure to a clearer way of viewing the world affects our thinking in fundamental ways. Learning to perceive truth is intrinsically rewarding, and we begin to seek it in experiences outside the dojo. Constant exposure to this kind of thinking can ultimately have a profound effect on our personalities.

"Spiritual" cleansing also comes from hard training. A tired body seems more inclined to operate in unity with the mind, leading to the kind of clarity that often follows intense meditation. At the extreme limit of fatigue, an exhausted body becomes unable to resist the dictates of the spirit. According to certain budo philosophers, there eventually arises a "perfect" relationship between mind and body, at which point the whole human being becomes a means of expressing divine intention, and thus is no longer constrained by ordinary physical and mental limitations. It is when students experience this oneness that they find their training most rewarding.

2

Training the Mind

There are few men who can reply quickly to the question, "What is the Way of the Warrior?"

—from *Hagakure*

Mental Discipline

There is no way to attain mastery of any martial art without using the mind. Mind and body are inseparable, and even if the conscious mind is doing nothing other than thinking, "I really hate doing all these front kicks," the unconscious mind is moving the body through the motions and making adjustments to fit the circumstances. Every action has an effect on every thought and every thought affects every action. This is why it is so important to take active control of the mind in the dojo.

Because budo training can be so repetitious, many students daydream their way through practice. Do not allow yourself to fall into this trap. Daydreaming saps the body of energy and ends up making practice even harder. Force yourself to concentrate on the techniques, constantly finding new aspects to work on. When you feel tired during practice, push yourself past the fatigue and train even harder. You will find that the more you commit to hard practice, the more energy you will have available for it.

Negative thoughts perpetuate themselves. Avoid complaining or even allowing the idea of complaint to arise. Do not disagree with your instructor during class. If you feel that something is wrong in your training, reflect on it fully and carefully outside the dojo. Do not bring it through the doors as a complaint, even in your mind, unless you are absolutely confident about your position. Even then, bring it up in private with your instructor, and tread lightly. If you have put the proper effort into seeking out good instruction in the first place, the chances are good that the teacher has sound reasons for doing things a certain way.

Be very reluctant to criticize anyone or anything in the dojo, except yourself. This approach is good for practical reasons, since it allows things to run smoothly, but there is an even more important reason for it. It helps to turn your critical focus inward, forcing you to accommodate yourself to circumstances. In daily training, you will be thinking about how you can improve, so eventually you will get better. In a fighting situation, you will adapt to the attack, giving yourself a better chance of avoiding it and countering.

This last point is one reason why it is so dangerous to practice martial arts using weak, choreographed attacks. Removing too much vigor from the attacker's role trains us to be weak. We may begin to focus on the fact that our partners are not attacking us "right," so we cannot execute our techniques. This is dangerous thinking; after all, it is ridiculous to imagine a real attacker stopping to adjust his grab so that we can easily release our arm and throw him. When someone tries to hurt or kill us, we must use any means available to escape or defend ourselves, whether they fall into the cannon of "correct" technique or not.

None of this means that we ought to give up independent thinking because we are involved in martial arts. Budo training can be a tool to help us become more incisive thinkers, but there is a time and place for the exchange of ideas, whereas the dojo is meant to be a place for practice of ideas disseminated mainly by the teacher. Experience has shown that the best martial artists are those who understand this distinction and put it into practice.

Every Action Becomes a Habit

Whether you practice your kata correctly tomorrow or just go through the motions, you will have spent the same amount of time in the dojo. In the first case, you will have moved one step closer to mastery of the kata, but in the second case, even though you have gotten a little exercise, you will have actually moved your training backwards. This is because, in the dojo, every action becomes a habit.

Building on a good habit is much easier than overcoming a bad one. It is said that if you practice a skill incorrectly one thousand times, you will need two thousand correct repetitions to learn it properly. This may be a slight exaggeration, but experience shows that most students who do not learn to monitor themselves and focus on practicing correct technique never get very good. If your training is worth doing, then it is worth doing right, and you will get much more satisfaction from it if you can see progress as a result of your hard work. The sooner you decide to make every training session better than the one before it, the sooner you will begin to make real progress.

Deepen Your Understanding

All techniques can be understood in a variety of ways. Kata can be studied from the point of view of physical movement, the principles by which the techniques work, timing, *bunkai* (the fighting application of the technique), history, and so on. A throwing technique may work according to a single specific principle, but you must also learn what differences will result from applying it at different angles or with different timing, how to defend against any variation, and even who invented the technique, and when and why, and the evolution it has undergone over time. The more you know about the technique, the better you will eventually perform it.

There are natural stages in the life of a martial artist, but it takes effort to move from one to the next. Time in practice is only one factor; far more important are intensity of practice and constant striving to know more about your art. If you work hard and are lucky, you will move from beginner to intermediate, and eventually to advanced student. To become a teacher is easy—you just start offering lessons—but to be a good teacher means that you must have a very deep understanding of the art.

Mastery of a martial art means that the technique and person are not separate. The art grows out of the artist, and the artist is a product of a lifetime's immersion in the art. It is popular in some circles to imagine that any person with a pure heart who is relaxed enough will perform perfectly, but this is wishful thinking. Only serious hard work with the body and mind will lead to mastery.

Observation

Although we are constantly looking at things, most of us do not see clearly. We have ears, but do not always hear correctly. We need to be taught how to observe. This becomes abundantly clear when a new student begins practice in the dojo. Shown a simple stance or hand movement, the new student will almost always leave out an essential part when executing it. After the second or third explanation or demonstration, the student will come much closer to adhering to the desired checkpoints. An advanced student, on the other hand, will do it almost right the first time, even if he or she has not studied the same martial art before. Novice students also have difficulty facing attackers in the dojo. They often focus on the wrong aspects of the attack and end up getting hit or kicked. After a longer period of training, of course, they do much better.

You can greatly improve your ability in both solo practice and in sparring or self-defense by teaching yourself to observe clearly. In budo, this means not only looking and listening carefully, but also making sure your body is following instructions. When an instructor tells you to pull your shoulders down, do more than nod your head. Consciously attempt to pull your shoulders down. If you are not sure how "down" should feel, raise them to see what that is like, then pull them down again. This sounds like common sense, but almost every instructor can tell you about students who listen to instructions, shout, *"Hai!"* (Right!), and then fail to do what has been asked of them.

During regular training, keep your eyes open. If the technique of a student near you seems weak, look carefully to see what he or she is doing wrong. You may feel satisfied if you simply recognize the problem, but to complete the learning process, mentally check yourself to make sure that you are not making the same mistake. Go further and study the stance and movements of your instructor. Rather than waiting for your technique to be corrected, consciously try to duplicate the teacher's movements, or those of senior students who are executing the technique properly. If you fail, it will then be because you either do not understand fully or are simply not capable of performing at the same level, but at least it will not be because you made no effort.

In time, observation and self-correction will become reflexive, and your learning process will accelerate. Another benefit of this sort of observation is that you will become skilled at judging people's ability simply by looking at them. Many great teachers can make accurate guesses about a student's past training and rank by watching them perform a single technique. There is no great mystery in this—it simply takes a long time to learn to do it. It comes from being aware of many people's strengths and weaknesses and observing how they develop during training.

Strong powers of observation will make you far better in the ring or when defending yourself. Besides knowing the telltale signs that allow you to predict certain attacks, you will also be able to discern the weaknesses of opponents as soon as they make their initial moves. If you learn both to predict the attacks of opponents and to exploit their weak-nesses, you will succeed far more often in competition.

Two-Sided Mind

Our goal in martial arts training is to learn skills that we can apply to all areas of our lives. Still, the outside world places different demands on us than does the dojo. Life as a martial artist will be much more rewarding if you can learn to separate these two worlds in your mind.

In the dojo, you are expected to work hard, obey the teacher, and be respectful to seniors. Your opinion is not particularly valued; only the instructor's opinion counts. When you are offered advice, you do not agree or disagree, you simply say, "Hai!" You call your seniors *sempai* and the head teacher *sensei*, yet they call you by your first name. Whatever your economic or social standing outside the school, where you stand in the dojo depends on how long you have been there and how hard you have worked. If you have a sensitive or artistic nature, you are expected to sup-press it during training. Pain, unless caused by serious dis-ease or injury, is supposed to be ignored.

Outside, your opinion counts. There are situations in which it is impolite or improper to express yourself, but in most cases your friends value your ideas. If others express themselves and you disagree, you feel free to explain how and why. Economic status has a large bearing on how you interact with others. At the same time, you are free to express your creative and sensitive side. Pain is something to be sympathized with, talked over, and treated.

Those who insist upon behaving as if they were in the outside world when they are in the dojo are just as foolish and misguided as those who insist that others follow dojo regulations in their outside lives. The correct principle to follow is to behave in a manner appropriate to the circumstances, neither overly familiar and unrestrained in the school nor sanctimonious and rigid at home. New students are most likely to cause awkwardness by failing to modify their conduct to agree with their locations.

Train hard when training, relax fully when taking time off. Jump to follow rules in the dojo, but don't be offended by the casual behavior of your seniors in their time off. Be careful not to treat a love relationship like a training relationship, since the rules are much clearer in the latter. Success in both the dojo and the outside world comes through hard work and clarity of purpose, although many of the rules and methods are different. Be sure to understand each environment and behave accordingly.

No-Mind

There is a state of being that is the goal of Zen training, called "no-mind." Our goal in martial arts is similar to this. We strive to become so proficient at our techniques that they happen without our conscious bidding, manifesting themselves at the right time, correctly executed, and achieving proper results. Many students believe that they must consciously suppress their intellect in order to reach this state, but in martial arts our approach is different. We try to reach a state of no-mind by forgetting about trying to attain it. As in every area of budo, the key to understanding no-mind is hard training.

By throwing yourself into your training, you become more and more skilled at your art. Techniques that were difficult at first become easier, then more difficult again as you find new aspects to practice. With time, an upward spiral of learning takes place. Eventually, some techniques become reflexive. If you practice enough, there will be occasions during which you will be attacked when you are not expecting it, and your body will act out its trained response. Your aim in training should be to develop all your techniques to this level, which is a lifetime's work.

Some students misapprehend the idea of no-mind in a

way that results in their becoming lazy. They choose to adopt a state of mental passivity, thinking that this is somehow close to the desired condition. As with most excuses to avoid hard work, this takes the student away from good technique and incisive thinking, making it harder to excel rather than easier. Stop yourself from being lazy in training, mentally and physically, as soon as possible. If we assume that you are in the dojo because you want to be good at budo, doesn't it make sense to work for progress rather than to stagnate?

3

Budo Culture

*Purity is something that cannot be attained
except by piling effort upon effort.*
—Yamamoto Tsunetomo

About Budo Culture

People who practice budo are members of a special group.
They are seekers after truth, people who want something
more from life than a paycheck and a nice home. Their
abilities allow them to make unique contributions to their
communities and to the world. Unfortunately, there are
many misconceptions about budo, held by nonpractition-
ers and martial artists alike. Because of the incomplete or
poor education of many of our so-called masters, martial

artists are often seen as aggressive people, overly concerned with fighting and winning. While these stereotypes may often be true, they are not reflective of the ideal martial artist.

We need regular reminders of the high standards that we must set for ourselves. Since we set out to learn unique and dangerous skills, we must have a code of behavior that ensures we do not use those skills for wrongful purposes. Such a code, *bushido* (literally, "the way of the warrior"), has existed in Japan for centuries, but it is sometimes difficult for modern Westerners to understand how the antiquated and sometimes odd-sounding rules of this code apply to them. In the few places where they have been written down, these rules are enmeshed in an enormous amount of information about the culture that gave birth to them, which can make it difficult to understand their practical value. It is helpful to study how they are applied and to determine their purposes if we want to know how and why we should follow them today.

Many Western students of budo believe that a moral or social code is a waste of time, assuming that physical practice is the only thing that will help them make progress in their chosen art. In fact, the nonphysical qualities of good martial artists—such as sincerity, politeness, loyalty, honor, and courage—are qualities that actually help them succeed. Martial arts practice, like most human endeavors, is a social act, and none of us can succeed without a great deal of contact with other people. The rules of bushido govern our interactions with those people—our teachers, our peers in the dojo, competitors, and the junior students whom we help. Our egos are exposed in practice by encounters with fear and pain, and bushido helps to provide a buffer against the conflicts this might create.

Sincerity

In martial arts, as in life, you are expected to mean what you say. This is simple to understand when it is a matter of expressing your intention. If you say, "I am going to practice this technique one thousand times," then everybody who heard you say it will think less of you if you quit after six hundred and fifty repetitions. The simple rule in such a case is: If you are not sure you can do it, don't say anything. In all matters in the dojo you are expected to be sincere. This extends to the smallest action or word. When you bow to show respect for the masters, it will be an empty gesture unless you know something about them and why they are worthy of respect. If you are thinking about your work when you bow, the bow is insincere.

Similarly, using the word *sensei* has an important role in your training. Your teacher gives you all the most important building blocks in your martial arts career, but many students forget this after a few years. These students begin to imagine that their ability is entirely due to their own greatness. You should always use the word *sensei* with respect and affection in your heart. This will help you view your relationship with your teacher in the proper light.

You must monitor yourself to make sure that your training aims are appropriate. Training just to earn a promotion or to impress someone in the dojo will cause you to veer off the path. No teacher can read your mind, but eventually your actions will demonstrate where your heart lies. The sweat and intimacy of training guarantee that sooner or later you will reveal your true intentions to your teacher. Before you begin to act upon these incorrect goals, they will have begun to develop in your mind. The time to root them out is early, when they first appear.

Sincerity is a powerful tool in your training, because it allows you to act without hesitation. Insincere actions and words destroy confidence and cause hesitation; these problems are deadly to a martial artist. Mental weaknesses translate into physical shortcomings. Next to prolonged training, simply deciding on a course of action and carrying it out with total commitment can improve your skill in the dojo tremendously. I have seen this over and over again in my students.

Sincerity means matching word and deed, but in budo it means more than that. It means matching word and deed with state of mind, or with the intentions of your heart. We are not often taught this, because it is a much harder way to live, but the satisfaction of acting with a unified mind, body, and spirit cannot be compared with any other reward.

Courtesy

The dojo is a place where there are many chances to hurt other people, physically and emotionally. Uncontrolled punches and thoughtless words can both cause injury, so all students must learn caution in these areas. Good manners smooth the rough edges of practice, and good control of technique is nothing more than the extension of the same principle into the physical realm. You must show regard for your training partner at all times.

What may seem like an empty ritual is more often an important component of training. For example, we do not allow our students to walk between two other students who are talking or practicing together. The physical awareness of the personal space of others is crucial in budo, and it makes no more sense to unconsciously walk between two training partners in the dojo than it would to carelessly get between two people who are fighting on the street. If crossing between them is unavoidable, we extend our right hand out and down, which is the nonverbal Japanese equivalent of saying, "Excuse me." By borrowing the Japanese hand gesture, we are linking a rule of common courtesy to a physical movement, which helps students to remember it.

The rules of almost every dojo require that students who are bowing in a line wait for the senior students to rise from the bow first. This follows the rules of respect for rank, but also helps develop awareness, peripheral vision, hearing, and tactile awareness. It is a mistake to think that the training starts only after the bow is complete. Every action in the dojo, from paying dues to free sparring, should be a training exercise.

Budoka vs. Budoman

Among martial artists, the words used to describe people hold a special importance. How you refer to someone can have a great impact on how others perceive that person. When deciding whether to attend a seminar, for example, it is not uncommon to query other martial artists about the teacher to find out what he teaches, what his background is, how skilled he is, and if he is a competent instructor. The skill levels at a certain rank are so variable from school to school that it is not enough just to hear that such and such a teacher holds a seventh-degree black belt or a teaching title.

Two terms used to distinguish between different types of martial artists are the suffixes *-ka* (Japanese for "person" or "profession") and *-man* (the English word). These follow the name of the martial art practiced by the person under discussion, as in *karateka*, *aikidoka*, or "judoman." *Karateka* means a person who has devoted him- or herself seriously to the art of karate, the aikidoka to aikido, and so forth. On the surface, both the -ka and -man endings have essentially the same meaning (-man being coined in English when few women practiced martial arts, so no corresponding female suffix has yet come into common use), but in actual usage they connote a very different sort of person.

Even though the -ka ending is taken directly from Japanese, in English it is often used to refer to a martial artist who puts on airs. Thus, the use of aikidoka, karateka, or judoka implies that someone is more concerned with form than substance, imagines himself a real samurai warrior somehow transported into the twenty-first century, prefers talking about himself to training, or thinks that his spirit is strong even though his techniques are weak. It is difficult to say how this usage evolved, but it may have something to do with the awkwardness of using terms from another language.

A budoman, however, is usually a person who is strong in technique and in body. Because these traits are most desirable in judo and karate, you are most likely to hear people praise the attitude and technique of a judoman or a karateman. Since softness and harmony are more valued in most types of aikido, you are less likely to hear someone described as an aikidoman.

Typically, the more exalted or historic the term, the more ridiculous it sounds to people who understand budo. Calling someone a samurai in an English-speaking country is a form of ridicule, and makes no more sense than would calling someone a knight. Master, as in "he is a karate master," usually means either the speaker or the person being spoken about doesn't have a clue about real karate. *Shihan*, a term that refers either to an instructor or a master instructor, depending on the context, is often overused. Knowing the dictionary definition of a word does not mean that one understands how to use it properly. Be very cautious about using Japanese expressions in your conversations.

PX Rangers

PX is short for "post exchange," a sort of general store on a military base. The term "PX ranger" is used to refer to a soldier who hangs around the base telling others of his exploits in the field. Of course, the stories are usually fictional. In martial arts, we might call such people "beerhall budomen." These sorts are far too common, and can often be found lurking around martial arts seminars or tournaments. There are several easy ways to identify them.

The first notable characteristic of beerhall budomen is their affection for emblems, patches, embroidery, and certificates. They seem to like nothing better than to stand in a crowd of martial arts students, pointing to their decorations and explaining the significance of each. A black-belt patch will be sewn onto their uniform below a sensei patch, above which you can find *dai-sensei*, "champion," and "chief-instructor." These people attend special events mainly to add to their collection of ego-gratifying paraphernalia.

Another way to identify people who like the aura of martial arts training better than the training itself is to watch during seminars classes. They usually find a way to avoid most of the serious training, either by going to the bathroom after the first twenty minutes of the seminar and returning just in time to bow out at the end, or by finding the weakest looking beginning student in the room and spending the entire class with him. If you see someone deliberately or frequently avoiding hard work, you can be pretty sure he is a member of this group.

It also seems that the people who do the least work try to grab the most attention outside the dojo. After noticing someone who avoids training in a few classes, watch that person in the cafeteria or bar afterwards. Note that the jaw muscles will be getting plenty of exercise now that the threat of serious training is past. You will find these folks sucking up to the head instructor while he tries to enjoy his postworkout beer in relative peace and quiet.

These slackers do have some usefulness in martial arts. They help to increase the total number of students who attend seminars, making it possible to host events that might otherwise be too expensive. They provide entertainment, if you care to listen, by unconsciously playing the fool (nothing they say matches what they do). They also make the serious martial artists look good, since their skill level never rises above what they can achieve in twenty minutes of basic practice per week. The one danger they pose is that some students will believe their stories and hold a falsely high opinion of them, or pay them to teach, but luckily most martial artists eventually come to see the truth about beerhall budomen, and learn to listen with a skeptical ear.

Wear a White Belt

Whenever you go to a new dojo to train, wear a white belt. This shows that you have a sincere desire to learn, and that you are willing to put aside your preconceptions. This point of etiquette is fairly widely known, but many people ignore it, either by actually wearing a colored belt or by failing to enter the dojo with an open mind.

The best possible impression you can make by wearing

a belt showing your rank from another school into the dojo is that you are confident in your rank and would be willing to participate in all of the activities expected of people of that rank at that dojo. If these activities include *kumite* or *randori* (free fighting), you may be expected to spar with others of equal or greater rank. Don't be surprised if a special sparring session is arranged just to see how good you are.

A more likely interpretation, however, will be that you are poorly trained, because you do not know the rule about wearing a white belt. If your skill level does not match that of the students in that school (and how could it, unless you have trained in exactly the same martial art they do?), then you will also be seen as unskilled. Any protestations you make about your training having been different will sound like whining. You can avoid all this by following the white-belt rule.

A closely related problem, more serious than wearing a colored belt, is the student who enters a new dojo carrying all the baggage from his or her past training. This student wants to learn what the new school teaches, but does not want to put aside the ways of his last teacher. The end result is that both sets of skills, the new and the old, suffer in quality, and the new teacher wonders why the student is asking for instructions but not following them.

Another similar problem can arise among students who stay in one dojo to achieve high brown-belt or black-belt ranks. They come to think that the relatively high rank they possess means they now know everything. They stop listening to their teachers, forgetting that it was the teachers who gave them the tools to get as far as they have.

In truth, every student must wear a white belt, either actually or internally, at all times in the dojo. The act indicates a willingness to learn, which is our purpose in studying martial arts.

4

Three Martial Virtues

*Perceiving what is right, and not doing it,
argues lack of courage.*
—Confucius

Strength

There are three major types of strength in budo: physical strength, strength in technique, and strength of character. The power of the body is the most basic type, since it is the easiest to develop and all of us have some strength to begin with. Technique is more difficult to develop because it involves overcoming natural responses and, through training, replacing them with reasoned ones. Strength of character is the most important of these three qualities, and budo is based on the idea that the way to improve character is mainly through hard work in the other two areas.

A long period of arduous physical training (measured in decades, not weeks) is necessary to master technique and to train the mind. Though great masters such as Yamaoka Tesshu and Ueshiba Morihei said that a unified spirit was the single most important quality for a martial artist, both men, and many other acknowledged masters, spent thirty or forty years in extraordinarily hard physical practice before reaching that state known as "enlightenment."

The martial artist must be physically strong because all technique is based on movement of the body. In order to persevere through the daily hours of practice, one must have endurance; to wield the sword properly, one must have strong arms; to kick well, the leg muscles must be able to easily lift the leg repeatedly into the air. Through strength training, one also develops coordination.

Technical prowess is important in self-defense because we always run the risk of meeting an opponent physically stronger than ourselves. It is also important because our skills, especially those based on muscular strength, lose effectiveness as we grow older. Also, we gain strength of character through the very process of studying and improving our skills. The knowledge and humility that come through lengthy practice are crucial aspects of character development.

Cultivating a strong character is essential because training is sometimes difficult and frustrating. It's also necessary because the skills we learn can make us overconfident, and because right action requires a strong will. Strength in this area is valuable, both to us and to society, because it allows us to follow through on our good intentions.

The way of the martial arts is to build strength through daily practice. Start within the limits of your capabilities, gradually increasing your own demands on yourself, and practicing every day. Study those more advanced than you to find out what you need to do to improve, and read about past masters for inspiration. This method applies to each of the three areas described above.

Physical strength can be increased in isolation, through a program of calisthenics or weight lifting, or it can be increased in conjunction with the development of technique. The way to develop them together is simply to practice each technique many times, attempting to improve gradually, while increasing the number of repetitions to fill the time available. Few students of the martial arts become experts only by attending classes, because there is not enough practice time within class hours. Most teachers utilize their class time for valuable lessons on skills and principles, and cannot include sufficient practice time, so it is the students' responsibility to seek out such time for themselves.

It is a mistake to want or to expect expertise overnight. Trying to reach too lofty a goal in a short time leads to failure, because neither the body nor the mind are prepared for the effort. In traditional martial arts, we can learn to move mountains, but we follow the method of moving them bit by bit, in amounts we can carry safely.

Developing strength of character is a natural result of correct training, but most of us need to pay special attention to right action. In training, part of right action means admitting that some of our techniques are not as good as others, and taking the time to work on them until they improve. It also means being truthful about the results of our techniques and realizing that, although they may work in certain practice situations, they may not be as powerful as we sometimes believe they are, and thus they need ever more work. Failing to be self-critical in this way can severely limit your growth as a martial artist.

An example of this kind of failing occurs in some aikido schools, which tailor attacks to fit the defensive technique being taught. Attacks are mounted from weak or off-balance positions and attackers fall without really being thrown. Instead of practicing and refining their techniques to be effective against truly strong attacks, students learn only to ward off weak, staged attacks, and thus can never develop effective defenses. This travesty of martial arts instruction is justified by the assertion of some instructors that aikido is supposed to be harmonious, but the approach bankrupts the art of its true value as a teaching tool. It also places students in serious danger of having their skills fail them when confronted with a real self-defense situation. Real technique is technique that works, and though we try to practice safely, we must never totally remove the martial underpinnings of our arts. If a proven technique does not work for us, we must deepen our study of it until it does, rather than diluting the attack to make the technique seem successful. Teachers at these schools do not seem to realize that, though self-criticism can be uncomfortable, the very process of overcoming our weaknesses is what makes us stronger—in body, in technique, and in character.

Outside of training, we need to cultivate right action in daily life, consciously choosing to do that which is honorable, necessary, or right. When given an opportunity to cheat, we must refuse it, knowing that cheating can become a habit. When faced with an unpleasant task, we must think through to the importance of getting it done, and overcome our reluctance to complete it.

The higher one rises through the ranks of martial artists, the more important this last characteristic becomes. Because the path of martial arts is so difficult, newer students often try to find ways to making it easier, and those ways include shirking their duties, blaming others for problems, and self-delusion. It falls to the senior students to correct their juniors, and almost nobody enjoys such work. Still, the necessity for doing it is clear, since a dojo would become chaotic and dangerous without good people management. The best students get the job done. By doing the necessary but unpleasant tasks, they learn about the rewards of correct action, some of which are greater control, a clearer conscience, and a better perception of truth.

There are many pitfalls on the path to becoming stronger. At the first sign of strength in themselves, many students experience an explosion of ego. They assume that since they are stronger than they once were, they are stronger than everybody, and this delusion can turn them into bullies. At the least, these students will find themselves stagnating until they can adjust their sense of themselves to fit their new abilities. At worst, they will become such bullies that they will have to be removed from the dojo.

Inflated egos are a problem for teachers of the martial arts as well. For those in positions of leadership, many of the ordinary avenues for feedback are removed. Most students do not dare attack their teachers with their best effort, and teachers can set up practice situations to give themselves the advantage. Being the biggest fish in a small pond is rewarding, but all of us in the martial arts must remember just how large the pond really is, and how many centuries of work by previous generations of teachers went into preparing the way for us. Keeping our proper place in mind helps to keep the ego in check.

Those martial artists who spend enough time and sincere effort developing themselves will find that they have improved their strength in each of the three areas. It usually turns out, however, that the goal of mastery does not look quite the same from higher up the ladder as it did from the bottom rung. There is, in fact, always as much more ladder above as there is below, since strength is a relative term. One must learn to accept the fact that perfection is an elusive goal. One may work hard to overcome certain weaknesses and find that progress has been made, but also find that constant work is required to maintain those gains. New problems often arise to replace those overcome. The increased responsibility that comes with higher rank often vexes students, who find that they have to balance the problems of the dojo and its members against matters related to their own training.

Long experience in martial arts practice will show us that our only real competition is with ourselves, but some students cannot overcome the desire to compete against others. They may become strong and skilled, but find that others are still stronger and more skilled. Instead of letting this discourage them, successful martial artists will learn to use this fact to motivate themselves to continue practicing and improving. After enough years, if they practice hard, have a good teacher, and are lucky, the practitioners' techniques will improve enough that they will work even against larger and stronger opponents. This kind of success helps them see through the keyhole of the door leading to the real meaning of budo.

Because success with technique helps motivate students to further pursue good technique, they should become more effective in a range of skills over time. Ironically, however, even the goal of perfecting technique can impose barriers to progress; those who fixate on one technique or one level of difficulty will stop progressing, while those who learn to seek out new methods and improve themselves will continue to grow.

Past masters have told us that, eventually, for a few of the best and most dedicated students, the pursuit of technique will become unnecessary, and they will learn to triumph using force of will. Ueshiba was said to have reached this stage near the end of his life, though he never quit practicing. Yamaoka was supposed to have been unbeatable after several decades of practice, and he attributed this to a "unity of spirit" gained through long toil.

These days, in fact, many claim to have come near to this state, or to have reached it. As nice as it would be to believe that many martial artists are reaching enlightenment, I personally remain skeptical. My experiences training with many of the best and renowned masters lead me to believe that even the most fantastic feats these men and women perform are still just techniques, albeit remarkably well executed, rather than "pure spirit."

What this means for the future of our own practice is twofold. First, we must be very careful about accepting claims of greatness by the people we meet, and, second, whenever we begin to think we have reached perfection ourselves, we must remember how much longer and harder other living masters have worked—and that, if they haven't liberated themselves from physical reality after all their years of work, we probably haven't either.

It is still possible, however, to believe in the possibility of greatness, and the nobility of staying on the path toward it. The fantastic skills of the greatest masters are worthwhile goals in themselves, and studying to reach their level is made even more exciting by the possibility that something transcendent might lay just past our next thousand repetitions. We must constantly challenge ourselves to improve, every minute of every training day. If we honestly evaluate our strength, technique, and character, and improve each of them by small increments every day, we will sooner or later accomplish something great.

Courage

Courage is the cornerstone of the martial artist's character. Without it, he or she will never undertake all the training needed to become a great technician, or develop great moral strength. It is not a common quality, but it can be developed with the right kind of training regimen.

The most obvious sort of bravery found in martial arts is that needed to face an opponent's punch, kick, throw, or sword cut, but a much broader view is needed to understand the entire role of courage in budo. It takes many forms, but always has the purpose of keeping students on the path of right action, or getting them back on it if they have strayed.

For many, it takes courage just to enter into martial arts training at all. Going into a strange school and admitting that one is ignorant requires a type of bravery. There is also courage in the act of placing one's own welfare in the hands of another, such as a teacher or another student. Teachers of the martial arts need courage to take on the financial risks of opening a school, and of exposing themselves to the judgments of their students and other teachers.

But these are examples of the minor kinds of courage that we expect from the martial artist. Real courage, the kind that must be cultivated through training, is inseparable from right action, and nearly always contains a strong element of self-sacrifice. In feudal times, a samurai was expected to give up his life for his lord without a moment's thought. Nowadays, we must think for ourselves, but when there is action to be taken, we must still take it with the greatest commitment.

The threat of death shines a bright light on courageous people, and one can read many stories of great warriors who calmly faced their own impending deaths. While these stories show the result of a long period of hard training, the real sources of courage are the countless small challenges of everyday training. Without facing these smaller problems directly, we cannot learn to handle the larger ones. Just as when we cultivate strength, we build up to extraordinary levels of courage by starting with ordinary ones.

In terms of cultivating physical courage, this process is easy to understand. It would be unreasonable and dangerous to try to defeat a national judo champion on our first day on the mat, and any sensible student would feel fear at the prospect of trying to do so. Our entire first year would be better spent learning how to fall safely, how to maintain balance, and how to overcome the fear of being thrown. After two or three years, if we are talented, we might profit from a match with the national champion, but we could not reasonably hope to pose any kind of challenge to him for several more years. The quality we would demonstrate by trying to beat a champion judoist on our first day in the dojo would not be courage, but stupidity. In such a case, the amount of courage we possess should be inseparable from the amount of time we have spent in training. The usefulness of the relationship between the two is clear; the greater courage needed to calmly face more difficult challenges comes through extended training.

Stories of warriors giving up their lives for their lords may be helpful, though, to understand when self-sacrifice is actually courageous. The principle behind those historical loyalties was that the actions of the warrior helped to further the good of the community. A leader, who probably had a broader view of the situation, would tell the warrior what was needed to win a battle, and the warrior would obey because victory would help all his clansmen. The possibility of death was considered a necessary risk to support the overall good, and, should he actually be killed, his family would rejoice at his contribution even as they grieved for their loss.

In today's society, people identify so little with their families and employers that they can rarely be counted on to take actions that will help the larger cause. There are many reasons for this, mostly social and economic, but a population more willing to "do the right thing," even at some personal risk, helps our country become a better place to live.

In the dojo, where these social and economic factors are not in play, what constitutes an act of courage is much clearer. Not flinching when facing a punch is a basic and irrefutable example of courage that must be learned by every karate student. Having the fortitude to stand up and be thrown again and again until a technique no longer inspires fear is essential. Confronting a troublemaker and enforcing the school rules is necessary to the smooth running of the dojo, and requires bravery.

All these examples of courage arise out of an understanding that there is some purpose greater than the immediate threat. One learns not to flinch at a punch because an opponent would recognize weakness in it and follow up the attack with other, more effective, punches. One gets up many times to be thrown again because that is what is required to learn how to avoid being thrown in the future. The dojo member who disciplines his juniors does so because he values a safe, positive training environment more than he fears the juniors' displeasure.

Seeing the larger picture helps to diminish the emotional relevance of the minor discomforts. Over time, something as intimidating as a punch recedes in impact to its true value as a tiny element of a complete training life, and we can then deal with it calmly. This learning process is a vital part of character development in the martial arts. In training, we expose our students to fear-inspiring events, starting with the very small and the physical, and gradually raise the stakes, introducing more complex events and encounters that inspire fear on an emotional or moral level. These events cause fearful reactions at first, but little by little students come to understand their relative importance, and to handle them with calm and discipline.

The assumption we make, of course, is that learning to handle specific fears will eventually lead to a general equanimity, and it often does. Even the best teacher, however, can only take a student so far, and few students ever seem to overcome all fear, as legends lead us to believe that some past masters did.

In fact, the idea that one can lead a satisfying life without fear is questionable, since fear may often be a strength associated with caring. Understanding this, our goal is not to make our students into killing or dying machines. Though we do want to teach students to overcome their fear of personal, physical risk, we would be doing them no favors if we taught them not to care about their loved ones or their friends.

I can say from personal experience that nearly four decades of hard practice does help to reduce the fear of danger, but does not produce the kind of iron-headedness that one would expect from a robot warrior. One learns, instead, to put dangers in their proper perspective, to care deeply about important things, and to take action to protect those things, whether that action causes fear or not. Adopting a broad perspective and doing what is right shows real courage. Right action very often involves giving up something personal for a greater good; the great martial artist is ready and willing to do so.

Loyalty

Loyalty is the glue that connects the martial artist to his school, his family, and to all of society. We have already seen that courage with no good cause is not courage at all, and since all good causes are related to issues larger than ourselves, we must have a sense of our connection to them. If we recognize and accept that connection either overtly or intuitively, we will develop loyalty.

The dojo is an excellent place to foster the development of loyalty. Many students enter a dojo for very personal reasons, such as a desire to learn self-defense or to become more fit, but those who end up staying often do so because they feel a sense of family there. That sense of family is exactly what we hope will develop in students, since it will make it easier for them to follow the instructions of their seniors and will help them through times when they are frustrated with their training. Students who love and respect their teachers make the best training partners because they will execute techniques willingly and with a spirit of enthusiasm, whenever they are asked to do so. Viewed from the outside, this devotion can seem misguided, even dangerous, and there are situations in which it is. An unscrupulous teacher might well be able to influence students to do something bad or illegal, but we must be careful not to assume an unhealthy relationship exists just because a teacher expects extreme devotion from his students.

There are times when a teacher will throw a student about like a rag doll, and a nonmartial artist might well wonder why a student would allow her *sensei* to treat her so badly. What such an observer would not realize, however, is that the student's willingness to commit fully to the interaction allows her to experience firsthand the most powerful techniques of the teacher. At the extreme boundaries of human perception and physical reaction time lies a close approximation of a life-and-death battle, with high stakes and with great emotional rewards. If the teacher is really talented and, together with the student, enters into the exercise with positive intent and commitment, there is nothing more rewarding than this kind of training experience. It can be almost spiritual in its intensity, and because of the sheer joy of experiencing it, the student will feel an even greater sense of loyalty once she has been shown these outer boundaries of skill.

Furthermore, experiencing the teacher at his best gives students something to aim for. They will realize how extreme the limits of skill are, and will see how much their own skills must be developed to reach those limits. This realization produces another kind of loyalty, since the teacher is the best guide for the student intent on following the path of budo. Once a student is committed to becoming a dedicated martial artist, he or she will stay with the teacher for a very long time.

Leading students to the point of such awareness is no easy task, however. In the first months or years of budo training, students are not aware that there can be any such reward from the experience of great technique. To them, training can seem like endless repetitive drilling and physical toil. Great techniques may seem awesome to them, and they may desire to perform the techniques themselves, but they will not necessarily experience the broadening of perspective that more advanced students will. Beginning students must take the rewards of martial arts training as

matters of faith, and they will persevere through the difficult first period of training only in proportion to how well
they can imagine what may lie in the future, their sense of
belonging to the group, and how much they enjoy training
for its own sake.

Loyalty opens the way for great possibilities in training,
and as we have seen, it can also be abused. For this reason,
it is important for beginning martial arts students to shop
carefully for a teacher. It has been said that it would not be
a waste of time to spend several years looking for a good
teacher, and it bears repeating here. A student should visit
many schools and ask many others about their experiences
with their teachers.

Once students choose a school, however, they must
commit fully to the training, following the orders of the
instructor and doing their best to perform perfectly the
skills they are taught, without asking a lot of questions.
The techniques of the martial arts cannot be transmitted
through words alone, nor can they be experienced in a few
moments of training, so students must allow themselves
enough time in practice to have a chance at seeing what
budo is really all about. No one who gives up after a few
months can claim to have really understood his martial
art, much less grasped the essence of budo. Loyalty, in the

beginning, consists of little more than following the rules of the school and believing the future holds something worthwhile.

Intermediate students of the martial arts should begin to feel that sense of belonging described earlier. Loyalty, for them, will mean not wanting to let down their friends and training partners. They should have had enough rewarding experiences in the dojo that their trust in the teacher is no longer based on faith, but on experience. They should realize now that it is possible for them to become much better by working hard and following the advice of seniors. Whether or not they are willing to do the necessary work will determine whether they advance past this stage or stagnate and eventually quit.

Advanced students of budo, who are usually assisting teachers in the running of the school, or at least helping teach some classes, must have some understanding of the meaning of reciprocity, which is practical behavior based on loyalty. They should realize that, although they owe much of their success to their own hard training, they could not have reached this point without the teacher. This realization should be reflected in their relationships with juniors, who will look up to them in much the same way as they look up to the teacher. Their actions are examples to others, and they should be aware that weaknesses in their comportment will diminish the loyalty of juniors. Their relationship to the head teacher is a model for relationships between themselves and juniors, so their loyalty now becomes a very practical means of enforcing discipline within the lower ranks.

Some mention should be made at this point of the fact that advanced students must often leave their home dojo to complete their development. A natural part of the close relationship between teacher and student is that some students will grow and eventually become relatively close to the teacher in ability. There will probably always be a difference in the depth of their understanding, since the most advanced 10 percent of knowledge in martial arts is far more difficult to achieve than the first 90 percent, but just as children nearing adulthood must challenge their parents and seek their own role in the world, so must students of the martial arts eventually become complete individuals by seeking independence.

While this separation might seem like a severing of the ties of loyalty, and in some cases it may end up actually doing so, it is a necessary step in the maturation of students. By testing their abilities in a larger arena, students will come to have a better appreciation of what their teachers have gone through before them. As long as the students remember that nothing in their martial arts careers would have been possible without the guidance of their teachers, they will understand their proper place in the continuing succession of martial artists.

5

Training the Spirit

*The basis of true training in swordsmanship
is to forge the spirit.*

—Yamaoka Tesshu

The Heart of Budo

Budo is more than just learning how to fight. As I have in-
dicated, real budo is a way of seeking and grasping the
meaning of life. It is a particularly good tool for this because of its long history of development and refinement by
people who understood that budo is a lifelong quest for
personal perfection. The Japanese penchant for organizing
and refining, applied to arts that naturally involve all aspects of a person, has created a razor-sharp spiritual instru-
ment that can cut right to the core of what is real or true.

Those students who are attracted to budo for these more serious reasons will find many unsatisfactory arts and instructors. Schools in which fighting is taught for its own sake will not help them progress in psychological and philosophical areas. On the other hand, those schools that practice only form without the fighting foundations of budo, also merit little respect. The discerning martial artist will look for a school that teaches a legitimate, traditional martial art form with both the fighting aspects and the internal aspects intact.

Finding a good school is only the first step, however, in a long journey with many detours and pitfalls along the way. Just as martial arts offer many benefits, they also pose many difficulties, both external and internal. On the physical side, there is the difficulty of certain movements, exhaustion from rigorous practice, and the pain of sore or injured muscles. On the mental side, there is fear, including the fear of failure or fear of an opponent's attack, as well as the frustration, discouragement, and even depression that can result from failure to make satisfactory progress.

In this regard, competitive martial arts are a double-edged sword, both helping us to develop ourselves, and creating barriers to progress. The challenge of pitting our skills against others can be an excellent teacher. It can show us where our skills are strong and where they are weak. It forces us to involve ourselves fully in the moment, helping us to cultivate a focused mind. Team competition can help build a sense of camaraderie among the participants. Unfortunately, competition can be so exciting that it can become the sole motivation for training. The desire to win sometimes replaces the more important goals of real traditional martial arts training. Students who care for nothing other than winning matches are out of balance. A good teacher must help them understand that real victory is something much larger than a drawing-room trophy.

Luckily, there are a variety of reality checks incorporated into traditional budo, as we shall discuss shortly. Once students understand what to look for, they will find implicit lessons in everyday practice. These lessons can be found in each of the physical, mental, and spiritual areas of budo. Good students will learn to pay attention to the indicators and adapt their training methods according to what those indicators reveal.

A wise teacher will remind students not to place too much emphasis on how they compare with others in the dojo. Budo's value and meaning change over time, depending on one's age and time in practice. While it may be perfectly reasonable for a twenty-year old to spend six hours a day in physical training, a fifty-year-old budoman may not recover quickly enough to practice for such extended periods, and a seventy-year-old practitioner may have to limit physical training still more.

The physical limitations of older students are not a serious problem, however, since the goals of each of these martial artists will be different. Whereas younger people may reasonably be concerned about the power of their punches and their skill in competition, mature practitioners will probably be more interested in studying the principles of movement in the kata or in applying the concepts of strategy to their lives and work. Martial artists in late middle age will likely begin to focus more on matters of the spirit, and teaching others may be more important to them than being able to perform extraordinary physical feats. Each martial artist sees the same art through a different set of eyes, and what it represents for one will not be the same as for another.

One aim they should share, however, is to continually deepen their ability to perceive the truth. In this area budo overlaps with Zen. Both teach that a state of suspended judgment, called *no-mind*, is best for a clear perception of reality. For the warrior, a state of readiness without a predetermined course of action in mind is best; this state allows one to react instantly according to the precepts of one's training. No-mind allows the Zen practitioner to see the truth, neither quickly adopting any established view of things, nor allowing personal biases to interfere with perception. Zen teaches right thinking for budo, and budo teaches right awareness for Zen.

Self-Delusion

There are countless obstacles to success in budo. The demands of daily life and the effort of hard training are difficulties we must all grapple with before we can attain any measure of skill. These problems are not insurmountable, however, and the lessons we learn in overcoming them actually enhance our ability to cope with the vicissitudes of life. The real difficulty lies in avoiding self-delusion.

Self-delusion can take many forms. In solo training, an example would be believing that you are executing a move correctly when in fact you are not. In sparring or competing, making up excuses for losing when your opponent was actually better than you is a form of self-delusion. In studying the philosophy of budo, you may think you are applying its principles to your own life, when really you are not. In truth, it is much more difficult to live by these principles than most students realize.

A teacher can only do so much with students who are willing to delude themselves. Experience has shown that students who do not quickly take action on their teacher's advice are unlikely ever to do so. Students must accept on faith that the teacher has a deeper understanding of the art than they do and vigorously apply themselves to their training. They must be willing to change. Every action becomes a habit, and putting off personal change, either in physical or spiritual matters, leads to self-delusion.

This self-delusion arises because change requires effort. Many students fall into the mindset that a technique is correct because it feels comfortable. This is patently untrue—any good teacher of martial arts can point out techniques that will always require extraordinary physical effort and mental concentration—but the extra work needed to change makes these students uncomfortable, so they justify staying put by telling themselves that they are doing the technique right. For students to admit to themselves that they have been corrected several times without having fixed their techniques constitutes an acknowledgment of their own stubbornness, which is painful. Many go on doing the techniques wrong rather than face their own weaknesses.

The concept of self-improvement in budo not only means that students should be trying to improve their character, but that they are responsible for putting forth the effort to do so. Those who rely solely on the teacher to guide them will never excel. Each student must constantly be on guard against false self-evaluation, and seek out the truth at every opportunity. Students who desire to become great in budo must face their weaknesses and actually seek out critical feedback, even when it makes them uncomfortable.

Finding out the truth is often simple. It may require nothing more than getting up in front of the teacher to perform, and asking for criticism and advice. Though different teachers have different personalities—some give more feedback and some less—students who take it upon themselves to succeed can do so regardless of the temperament and methods of their teachers.

Facing weakness can be as direct as standing up and trying again after being thrown many times. It can be candidly admitting that a winning opponent was faster, more skillful, or in better condition, instead of resorting to excuses. The truth can be painful, as on those occasions when one must continue to strike the makiwara in spite of bleeding knuckles, but whatever form this overcoming of self-delusion takes, it is something that serious martial artists must force themselves to face every day. Like all important and worthwhile endeavors, overcoming self-delusion requires daily commitment and perseverance.

What Is Real Victory?

Victory, to many martial arts students, means physical triumph over another person: a full-point throw in judo, an uncontested strike with a shinai to a vital area in kendo, or a karate punch that finds its target without being blocked. While these feats do represent a certain kind of victory, one that gives us a short-term sense of superiority over another person, *real* victory in martial arts is something different.

As in Zen, real victory in budo is mastery of the self—body, mind, and spirit. While defeating an opponent in a match tends to inflate the ego, serious study of budo over a long period of time helps to give one a realistic sense of one's place in society. Training only for fighting or for competition teaches valuable lessons in discipline, and is good physical conditioning, but it also exposes the athlete to great risk of injury. The study of traditional budo teaches the same lessons and more, but also provides for the safety of the practitioner, so that progress is less often interrupted by periods of recuperation.

Real budo conditions the body while teaching us to control our limbs, our breathing, and to some extent, the functions of our internal organs. Repetitive practice of fundamental movements allows us to obtain a degree of control over our bodies that few nonmartial artists can imagine, yet there are far more important reasons to become involved in budo.

One of these reasons is mental discipline. Proper training in martial arts can help us to develop greatly heightened powers of observation. It teaches us orderly thinking habits, which can be useful in our education, our careers, and our relationships. It teaches us mental balance, which makes us happier and more productive. Ultimately, it allows us to achieve a state of direct perception that Zen scholars and past masters of budo have called *no-mind*, a sort of alert meditative state that helps us become fully immersed in whatever we are doing at a given time.

Through history, legend, and positive example, budo culture provides a host of good influences for us. We are constantly exposed to beneficial ideas, such as the importance of sincerity, courage, and benevolence. We are taught to be courteous and to value the contributions of those who came before us. Honor and duty are considered inseparable from correct practice of martial artistry and, indeed, without those qualities, a martial artist may be little more than a trained ruffian.

While the outer edges of martial arts have been distorted by financial and sporting issues, the core of traditional budo remains an austere and reflective pursuit. There are few places left in our society where we can examine life without it being reflected through the lens of some television producer or ad agency's idea of what might sell a product. Alone in the dojo with a two-hundred-year-old kata and the limitations of your own body, there is little room for romantic notions of short-term gain, yet what you take with you when you leave the dojo has value in a way that nothing you can pay money for ever will.

We must never forget the value of sweat and the pleasure of hard training, but real victory in the martial arts is more than simply a matter of progress in improving ourselves physically; it is rather the successful application of time-tested principles of budo to living a productive life. Health, benevolence, and contributions to society are essential characteristics of the advanced martial artist, just as much as are skill in performing kata, depth of understanding of principles, and fighting ability. Real victory is always just out of reach, since its shape changes as we grow older and more mature, but in striving for it every day we succeed in living more meaningful lives.

Reality Checks

For those who want to avoid straying too far from the path, budo provides a host of reality checks. These reality checks exist in the physical, mental, and spiritual realms. They take various forms, but they share one characteristic: all are accurate indicators that a student is doing something wrong.

The most obvious sign of a problem is a technique that does not work. This might be a block that does not stop a punch, a joint lock that does not immobilize, or a throw that does not drop an opponent cleanly and without a lot of muscular effort. Students who wish to learn will notice the failure of their techniques and begin working to correct them right away. If they cannot determine the reason that a technique does not work, they will seek out the advice of teachers or senior students. Once they grasp the principle, they will practice regularly until the correct technique becomes second nature. They will not be satisfied with less.

Mental weakness creates problems in interacting with others and in the learning process. Students who do not think before they act will find that their actions are not worthy of the respect of others, and will not progress in their own practice. They must have a clear understanding of the consequences of their actions. Words and deeds in the dojo are closely scrutinized, making it all the more important that it is understood how things are supposed to be done, and why. In deciding what, when, and how to practice, students must think deeply about what kind of person they want to be.

It has long been said that good budo requires a unified spirit. In battles and in competition, this means that one must attack with one's whole being: body, mind, and spirit. In the dojo, it means that one must stop thinking about work, school, or family when practice starts and focus fully on the lesson at hand. Students who are unable to do this seldom make much progress in their training. When students notice that they are distracted during class, they must strive harder to concentrate on the lesson.

There is more to the matter of spirit in the dojo, how-ever, than focused attention. The best students are those who love the training for its own sake. For such students, the practice itself fulfills their desire for personal advancement. Their enthusiasm translates into hard training, and their movements are sharper and more powerful than those of students who are just in the dojo for the exercise. When students train without enthusiasm, just going through the motions, the teacher will be unimpressed. Those who notice any lack of enthusiasm in themselves should seek out ways to make their training more intense and rewarding.

Many of the problems that seem to take away from the fun of training are actually signposts showing us where we need work. Just as an oyster responds to the irritation of sand by creating a pearl, you can become a great martial artist by focusing on your defects, piling effort upon effort to eliminate them, and overcoming all the problems you face with determination and hard work. With every barrier you pass through, you will find that your sense of accomplishment deepens. Your perceptions will change, giving rise both to clearer insight and to new problems. These problems, in turn, lead to solutions that encourage personal growth.

Learning to listen to the warning signals will make you a better student of your art. When you find that a technique does not work well, actively root out the problem and do not rest until you have found the solution and have applied it. If the reaction of others to your behavior does not satisfy you, think about possible reasons. Many students are too interested in self-expression to realize that budo begins with self-denial. Creativity in budo is the expression of mastery, not the source of it. In matters of the spirit, remember that the pleasure of hard training comes from being fully involved in it. Training with skepticism or reservation breeds boredom and stagnation. All martial artists go through difficult periods in their training, but the ones who go on to be great are those who constantly renew their commitment to train with interest and enthusiasm.

Budo and Zen

During Japan's long feudal history, Zen became a vital component of budo. Crucial concepts in Zen were useful in the training of warriors, so they were adopted and passed on to subsequent generations. These concepts helped to create more efficient soldiers as well as more constructive members of society. Today, they can teach us to be better competitors (if we choose to compete) or aid us in our search for truth.

It is important, however, to understand what *Zen* means in the context of the martial arts, since the word is used in different ways by different people. The word describes a branch of Buddhism that relies largely on meditation to attain enlightenment. (The Japanese word Zen derives from the Chinese word *Ch'an*, which in turn comes from a Sanskrit word meaning "meditation.") Like many powerful ideas, however, Zen started out simple and gradually became more complex. Different sects came into being as the result of doctrinal disputes over correct theory and method, and successive generations of teachers imparted their personal influence to their particular sects. Over time, in many sects, ritual and group politics became nearly as important as the original practice. Formal Zen practice, complete with long hours of meditation and endless ritual, may well be valuable to its adherents, but it will not be of much use to the martial artist.

Practitioners of budo should seek out the fundamental concepts of Zen and apply them to their training. The concept most useful to us is that, through hard training and a continuing desire to deepen our awareness, we can develop a clearer perception of truth. The hyperfocusing of our attention and the fatigue that comes with hard training help to overcome obstacles to clarity created by our personal beliefs or biases. The onslaught of attacks in a sparring session overloads the senses, forcing us to release our grip on the small and the unimportant, and to assimilate sensory input without engaging the analytical mind.

For the warrior, this means much faster reactions to dangerous attacks. If he has trained properly, it also means much more effective responses, since clearer perceptions will allow him to make an accurate evaluation of the speed and intensity of the attack and to react efficiently without being paralyzed with fear or sloppy due to over-confidence.

Developing the Zen mind is exceedingly difficult, but the steps you need have already been set forth in earlier chapters of this book. Hard work, long-term commitment, and a desire to improve are vital. If you find a traditional martial art and practice it for three or four decades, you may attain it. On the other hand, some people are faster learners, and may manage it in a few years.

Ultimately, however, Zen mind is experienced only by those who are both hardworking and lucky, and not every dedicated student will achieve it. It is not always easy to recognize. Some may experience it and, because it seems such an integral part of ordinary practice, dismiss it as nothing more than the exhilaration of an especially good training session. A few of the characteristics of the Zen state are as follows:

First, actions seem effortless. We execute a throw, strike, or other move, and it works perfectly, without any conscious thought or any feeling of struggling to get it right. This state can only result from concentrated practice over a long period of time. The complex movements of the martial arts must be performed over and over again and constantly refined before they can be executed in such a way that approaches the effortlessness of Zen.

Second, we experience a sense of detachment from the performance. We feel as though we are watching ourselves performing from the outside. We are aware of what we are doing, but do not feel involved in it. Somehow, the motions are executing themselves, which is probably what led the ancient martial artists to attribute such actions to a divine source. In competition, winning and losing seem unimportant. There is a sense of "rightness" in doing the actions for their own sake. Zen teachers emphasize that one must cultivate detachment in order to achieve this state. Earlier chapters detailed how this is accomplished: through hard, repetitive training, aiming at something greater than ourselves, and consciously putting aside thoughts of personal gain.

Third, worries vanish. When the body, mind, and spirit are all focused on the same goal, there is no room for petty concerns. We experience inner peace, similar to that achieved through meditation or prayer, but we experience it while in action. It is easy to see how valuable this quality would be to the warrior. Rising above fear allows one to single-mindedly pursue victory, regardless of consequences.

Finally, we feel at one with the greater flow of the universe. When our actions flow from a source that is not ourselves, we sense how much a part of our environment we are. We are no longer separated from nature, but a part of it. Once again, this is a characteristic that is very valuable to the warrior who, being totally in tune with the flow of events, can respond to the actions of opponents even as the opponents conceive of them. Since both are part of the same larger consciousness (if one accepts the spiritual explanation of this phenomenon), the warrior in the Zen state of mind will always defeat the opponent who's not in it. The ordinary warrior thinks about what must be done before doing it, while the Zen warrior spontaneously acts properly.

The paradox of Zen is that the moment the warrior starts to reflect on this miraculous unity of thought and action, he divides them in two again, and is reduced to the status of an ordinary mortal—one whose thoughts are separate from his actions. In martial arts practice, this happens frequently. We experience a transcendent moment when a technique springs out perfectly from some hidden place, and become immediately self-conscious—delighted at our success and intent on repeating it. Of course we won't be able to repeat it until some time in the future when the correct level of activity and focus will again spontaneously create in us the proper state of being. It surprises us again, as it should, since we only experience it when we are fully concentrating on the technique being executed, and never when we are striving for transcendence as a goal in itself.

The more we practice, the more often we experience brief moments of perfection. We cannot become complacent, however, since we stagnate as soon as we stop striving, so the life of the Zen aspirant is one of constant struggle. We work harder every day for the rare payoff, and as soon as it comes, it is gone. Only a lifetime of work brings us anywhere near the state where we spend more time in the Zen state than out of it, and only one person in millions reaches the point where he or she is always in the Zen mind. In the Zen religious tradition, such a person is a fully realized being, called Buddha.

The Japanese Martial Arts

Choosing a Martial Art

IN ORDER to benefit from the principles put forward in this book, you will have to choose some art through which to absorb them. The traditional martial arts of Japan have a complete structure and philosophy built into them, which makes them ideal for the kind of study you are going to pursue. Although almost any martial art could be used to practice comparable physical techniques, the mental and social aspects that I discuss are unique to Japanese martial culture, and sometimes even in conflict with accepted social norms of other countries.

This does not mean that the martial arts of other countries have less inherent value, but none that I know of has the same complete philosophical and structural organization that is shared by all the Japanese arts. One point is certain though: most of the modern fighting systems made up and taught in the West, such as boxing or American "jujutsu," are missing a large part of what makes studying traditional martial arts worthwhile. I believe that the unique characteristics of Japanese budo make it worthwhile as a lifetime's pursuit, so the explanations in this book are based on the assumption that you do, or will, study a traditional Japanese martial art.

When seeking martial arts instruction, there are a few important points to consider. The first is that the instructor is usually far more important to your education than the particular martial art you choose. This would not be the case if martial arts teachers were generally of high quality, but there is tremendous variation in the knowledge and teaching style of teachers, even in Japan. It is commonly said that you would not be wasting your time even if you spent a year or two looking for the right teacher. That may be an exaggeration, but you should definitely make sure that your teacher is well educated in his or her art, and that he or she offers a safe, positive learning environment. Go and watch a class at the school you are thinking of joining, and pay close attention to the attitude and teaching style of the head instructor (or subordinates or senior students if the instructor is not teaching at the time).

When you visit a school, note if any of the students are bullies, either physically or emotionally. While it is natural for a few of the senior students to have strong personalities, a good teacher will not tolerate bullying. Hard training is expected, and some strong direction or cajoling is good, so don't let a little shouting scare you off, but be sure that it is moderated by a genuine concern for the welfare of the students.

Practical concerns, such as the location of the school and the convenience of parking, can also have a major effect on your training. Common sense will tell you that the easier it is for you to get to the dojo, the more likely you are to be there for training every day. There are plenty of impediments to success in the training itself, so if you are lucky enough to find two schools of otherwise equal quality to choose from, it is best to join the one you can get to easily.

Be sure to choose a martial art that suits your personality. If you have a competitive nature and like to sweat, a defensive martial art that emphasizes harmony, like aikido, might not be a good first choice. Judo or karate would probably be much better. If you have a quiet, introspective personality, a meditative art such as iaido might suit you well. If you like throwing and grappling rather than punching and kicking, choose judo rather than karate. If you have a strong desire to overcome a particular weakness, such as a fear of being punched, then you might want to face that weakness directly and choose to study karate. However, you are more likely to stick with an art that matches your personality than with one that you do not naturally enjoy.

Many people take up the study of a second art only after being involved with their first art for several years. They develop good basic movement skills and a love for training in their first art, so their second art is usually easier to learn. It is chosen from a base of experience, which means that it probably fulfills their expectations better than the first art may have.

Finally, the most important thing you must do is get started. In spite of what I have stated above, trying to find the perfect martial art while missing the opportunities for training can be a serious waste of time. There is no better way to find out if you are going to enjoy a particular type of training than to get in there and do it. If you don't like the art you have chosen, then at least you will have improved your physical condition and practiced some fundamental techniques of good body movement, which means that you will be better prepared when you do find one you like. Let's now look at some of the major martial arts, and consider some of the pros and cons of each.

Aikido

Aikido consists mainly of throwing techniques and pins that rely on joint locking. It is almost wholly defensive in nature. Most of the skills involve responding to an opponent's attack and redirecting the offensive energy in such a way as to unbalance and topple the attacker. Many of the techniques involve circular motions that first take you out of harm's way, then cause the attacker to lose balance. Practice can be very gentle, especially in schools that emphasize the idea of using *ki* (intrinsic energy) over physical strength. The main philosophical premise of aikido is harmony with the opponent, both in body and spirit. Older people or people who are not in top physical condition can usually practice this art safely, at least at the beginning levels.

Ueshiba Morihei created aikido by modifying many earlier Japanese jujutsu techniques and adding to them the idea of harmonizing with the opponent's movements. Ueshiba was a religious man who stressed spiritual development as much as, or more than, physical development—an emphasis that some of his successors have adopted and reinforced. Today, there are four major schools of aikido: *Hombu* (headquarters), *Aikikai* (which emphasizes, softer, more fluid movement), *Yoshinkai* (the most regimented style of the three), and Ki Society aikido (a very soft style that emphasizes ki development). Many aikido schools also teach aiki sword, jo (the four-foot staff), and tanto (short sword).

The benefits of studying aikido are many. Its relatively gentle physical exercise builds strength gradually. The cooperative practice means there are few injuries, and it allows people with a wide range of abilities to practice together. The movement drills can transform a clumsy person into someone who moves with grace and good balance. The dojo is usually a pleasant social environment where students cooperate to get things done, and the principles of the art can be a good tool for learning how to manage conflict.

The drawbacks of the art are mostly the converse sides of its unique strengths. Because training involves cooperation, it is possible to practice for many years without ever knowing if your techniques would actually work in self-defense. It is generally a less strenuous workout than other martial arts such as judo or karate, though two people who want to train hard can easily add power and speed to their training. Finally, there is a disturbing trend in many schools to remove all traces of realism from their training, using light, compliant attacks and jumping or falling before the technique can actually be applied. This type of practice, while almost totally safe, is closer to dance than to a real martial art, and bankrupts aikido of many of its most valuable qualities.

Iaido

Iaido is a type of Japanese swordsmanship. Practice is made up almost entirely of kata, or prearranged sets of motion designed to respond to a particular attack by another swordsman. A kata typically consists of a draw, a parry, a major cut, a blade-cleaning motion, and a resheathing. Practice is calm and quiet, since the most important feature of iaido is the development of *zanshin* (a calm, reflective mind). In iaido, the major difficulty to overcome is the extraordinary attention to detail required. This is another art that is popular with older people and non-athletes, since the relatively slow movements are not as taxing to the cardiovascular system as are the more active arts (though it is still extremely challenging).

The person most responsible for the creation of modern iaido was a man named Hayashizaki Jinsuke. He brought together many older styles of swordsmanship to create a system that was ideal for castle guards and sentries to use in defending against surprise attacks. The unique drawing motion in most iaido kata is designed to draw the sword, to parry an oncoming cut, and to cut the opponent, all in one motion. Iaido, perhaps more than any other martial art except *kyudo* (archery), develops a calm, clear mind in its practitioners. Some of the major schools of iaido are: *Muso Shinden Ryu*, *Muso Jikiden Eishin Ryu*, and *Shinkage Ryu*.

Iaido training builds arm and leg strength and provides a gentle cardiovascular workout. As stated above, it helps in the development of a calm, stable demeanor and, through attention to detail and continual refinement of the motions, orderly, precise thought patterns. It is not an art for those who are impatient or who desire great activity. Some younger people find the practice style a bit slow, and there is no form of direct competition in iaido. Watch out for poorly trained instructors, who teach the general pattern of the forms, but who do not understand the precise details or the reasons for them. Without these essential components, iaido has little to offer in the way of mental discipline, and would be an unrewarding art for most people.

Judo

Judo is quite popular and is practiced both as a martial art and as an Olympic sport. Its techniques include both throwing and grappling. The throwing techniques utilize many different parts of the body, including the hands, legs, and hips. There are also two groups of sacrifice throws (in which a person throws him- or herself to the ground in order to throw the opponent), one group with the body aligned with the opponent's body and one with the body at a right angle to the opponent's. In grappling, there are pins, chokes, and joint locks. In sport judo, competitors score points by cleanly throwing their opponents, by holding them down for a preset period of time, or by forcing them to surrender with a choke or joint lock. In dojo practice, a great deal of time is spent learning kata, the formal techniques, which inculcate the principles of balance, flexibility, self-defense, and physical fitness.

The creator of judo was Kano Jigoro, a man who was a great educator and an internationalist, long before it was popular for Japanese to look outside their own borders. Kano wanted to devise an effective physical education method, so he modified and regrouped many techniques from old systems of jujutsu and sumo to form judo. One of his early kata was in fact called "People's Drill for Efficient Use of Physical Energy," but the emphasis in judo has more and more shifted to the techniques used in competition and away from the idea of physical education for health.

Judo is probably the premier martial art for people who want to train hard. Nowhere are balance and strength more important, since judo techniques are applied in opposition to an opponent's grasp, and hence everything is done against resistance. Because of the emphasis on competition, judo is usually considered a young person's martial art, but in more traditional schools older people can also benefit from the training. Typically as one gets older and less physically able, more and more emphasis is placed on the practice of kata.

The most serious drawbacks of judo practice, especially in its modern form, is the risk of injury. Because participants use their whole strength in competition, there are many opportunities for bruises, muscle pulls, and dislocated joints. A good teacher, however, can do a lot to minimize injuries by making sure students are well warmed up, that their techniques are based on sound principles of body movement, and that the idea of winning doesn't totally supplant respect for the health of their training partners.

Jujutsu

Jujutsu is considered the mother of all Japanese martial arts. Once called *taijutsu* or *yawara*, jujutsu was a loosely organized system of attack and defense methods that included throwing, hitting, kicking, joint locks, and many other skills. Although modern practice centers around throwing, grappling, and joint locks, there are so many variations on the way jujutsu is taught that it is imperative to visit a class in order to decide whether the school is offering the type of training you want. There are large numbers of "jujutsu" schools in the West in which the instructors teach the general fighting skills they learned in the military, or simply made up. While the techniques taught at such schools can be effective, the teaching methods usually lack the philosophical basis of true traditional Japanese arts.

There were probably hundreds of family systems of jujutsu in Japan at one time, and a few of these have been preserved to this day. Still practiced in some areas are such systems as *Kito Ryu, Ten Shin Shin'yo Ryu, Daito Ryu Aiki Jujutsu*, and *Yagyu Shingan Ryu*. The International Martial Arts Federation (IMAF), based in Tokyo, offers a composite system based on techniques from many of these schools called *Nihon Jujutsu*, which simply means "Japanese jujutsu." It is taught by IMAF's director, Sato Shizuya.

Traditional jujutsu is a fascinating study, and the techniques can be excellent for self-defense. Depending on how classes are taught, the physical demands can range from fairly low to extremely high, which is another reason to visit a class before choosing a school. Like aikido, jujutsu occasionally veers off into an exercise in fantasy when the participants don't subscribe to hard training. In such classes, attackers provide no resistance to the counter techniques, or even anticipate them by moving into weak positions, eliminating most of the art's value as self-defense training.

Jujutsu has experienced a surge in popularity recently because of the success of some practitioners in competitive fighting events. While this popularity is good for dojo owners, who benefit from the large numbers of new students, those who are deciding on a martial art should realize that there is much more to jujutsu than the few techniques used to win matches. Traditional jujutsu comes from ancient Japanese roots, and contains formal elements—often in the form of kata—that can appear very esoteric, even odd looking. Also, most family systems are imbued with religious or spiritual concepts.

Another problem created by these matches is that some students expect that their daily practice will be just like the competitions they see. This is a problem common to all martial arts that are featured in the entertainment world. What is unseen, of course, is all the work that the competitors put in before their matches, most of which is grueling, repetitious drilling on fundamentals. A good ratio to anticipate if you are interested in competition is five hundred to one thousand hours of practice before your first competition, most of which will be spent learning stances, stepping, fundamental techniques, and the application of these skills. If you want to get your feet wet in the ring sooner than that, go to a nontraditional school that emphasizes competition.

Karate

Karate means "empty hand," and refers to a wide variety of martial arts styles based on strong stepping, striking, blocking, and kicking techniques. Most were invented or systematized in Okinawa, but there are good reasons to believe that earlier Chinese martial arts played an important part in their development. In the early part of the twentieth century, several early pioneers of karate helped to introduce it into mainland Japan, and from there it has spread all over the globe.

Though all are called karate, the arts that bear that name can be very different from one another. *Shorin Ryu*, one of the oldest styles still practiced in its original form, tends to have short, jackhammer-style punches and requires quick steps along an angle. It is a style that is well suited to the smaller Okinawan physique. *Goju Ryu* means "hard-soft school." It is unique in that its practitioners learn to absorb an opponent's punches by tightening their own bodies and using special breathing methods. Its stances are very strong and well grounded. *Shotokan* karate is one of the more popular styles, emphasizing deep stances and powerful punching. *Wado Ryu* is a less well known school that has an enormous range of techniques. In Wado Ryu, unique countering methods deter an attacker, and then multiple strikes are used to finish him off. *Kyokushinkai* and *Oyama Karate* are violent, competitive styles that emphasize practical fighting skills as much as, or more than, traditional kata.

There are many benefits to karate training, including excellent aerobic and muscular conditioning, the acquisition of self-defense skills, and, often, a solid grounding in the philosophy of budo. The basic movement skills learned in karate—how to stand with stability and direct power, how to turn with balance, how to move along angles—are extremely important in all martial arts, and for that reason karate is an excellent first martial art. In addition, the progressive training exercises practiced in most schools help you progress to advanced material smoothly, with minimal danger or frustration. Karate can also help you overcome a fear of being hit or kicked, and help you realize that a few bumps and bruises are not the end of the world.

Unfortunately, many karate schools emphasize sparring or competition to the exclusion of the more traditional aspects. While these activities are exciting, they are only a part of training; a school that provides kata practice and training in basic principles as well will develop much more capable students over the long term. Look for a school that emphasizes safety in practice and take note of how students move. If they appear ungainly or weak, especially at the higher levels, the teacher may not be teaching strong basic skills. Shop elsewhere for your training.

Kendo

Kendo means "the way of the sword." Students protect themselves during practice with padded armor covering the head, upper body, and hands, and score points against each other by striking designated areas with a *shinai* (a practice sword of split bamboo). Competition is fast-paced and exciting, but many hours of drilling are required before you can expect any success in sparring. There is also a kata element to kendo, using metal practice swords, in which students study and practice forms that are very similar to iaido forms.

Kendo is the most popular type of swordsmanship in Japan. Junior high school students there can join kendo clubs at their schools, and many continue to practice for the rest of their lives. The art is evolved from older swordsmanship styles, sometimes called kendo, but usually referred to as *kenjutsu* (sword art). These earlier forms of the art were practiced with wooden swords or real blades, but as the sport evolved and the use of the point system developed during the eighteenth century, it became too dangerous to use any solid weapon, and so the *shinai* was created.

This art is ideal for anyone who desires a good aerobic workout. Practice develops excellent muscle tone and improves mental focus. Muscular strength is a minor factor in winning matches, so men and women can compete equally, making kendo a good martial art for anyone. Factors that limit the appeal of kendo are the difficulty of finding good instruction outside of Japan, and the discomfort of the body armor. Another consideration is that there are no direct self-defense applications for kendo movements, so if your primary purpose in studying martial arts is self-defense, it would be better to choose another art.

Kobudo

Kobudo (literally, "ancient martial art") does not refer to a single art, but rather to a group of arts including *kenjutsu*, *iaijutsu* and *battojutsu*, *jodo*, *naginata-do*, *ninjutsu*, various old styles of jujutsu, the Okinawan weapons arts, and others. You cannot obtain a rank in *kobudo;* instead you study one or more of the specialized arts that are included in it, each of which has unique characteristics.

Iaijutsu and battojutsu are basically the same as iaido, though the techniques often retain more of the flavor of fighting techniques than Zen ritual. These systems also encourage cutting practice, using rolled straw mats or bamboo, whereas many iaido schools discourage cutting, claiming that such practical application of the techniques is unnecessary.

The jo is a four-foot wooden staff, and *jodo* is "the way of the staff." Techniques with the jo include striking, poking, parrying, and blocking. Some styles include joint locks and throws, which are executed against an opponent who grasps your weapon. Traditional jodo is highly systematized, with practice drills and kata, as well as individual self-defense techniques. Practice is active, but not nearly as intense as judo or karate.

Kenjutsu means "the way of the sword," but the arts with this name are distinct from iaido and kendo. In kenjutsu, wooden swords are typically used, rather than metal practice swords or shinai. These systems usually emphasize fighting techniques more than formalized kata, and are often much more active than iaido. Legitimate schools teaching kenjutsu in the traditional manner are very rare outside Japan.

The *naginata* is a long-handled weapon with a short, curved blade at one end. These days, the art of naginata-do is primarily practiced by women in Japan, though a few men do study it. Practice is much like kendo, with individual technique practice, kata, and sparring, with kendo armor and weapons that have short, split-bamboo blades like the shinai. Practice of this art can be quite strenuous, depending on how much the teacher enjoys hard work.

Ninjutsu means "the art of the assassin." Proponents claim that there is an unbroken tradition of techniques and philosophy dating back several hundred years, but this idea is in some dispute. Reputable modern historians say that the original *ninja* were disorganized opportunists, and that the idea of a classical system was created only recently to help promote the art. Ninjutsu practice involves stalking and hiding techniques, climbing, the use of explosives, small weapons, and almost any other skill that could be useful to an assassin. Students often wear black from head to toe, and much of the training is done outdoors.

There are six weapons considered to be the classical weapons of the Okinawan warrior. Most of these were adapted from farm implements and some were used to fight the Japanese invaders of Okinawa, who forbade the Okinawans to use swords. A system of defensive techniques and one or more kata was devised for each weapon. The six classical weapons are the *rokushaku bo* (six-foot staff), the *sai* (short, pitchfork-like weapons), the *tonfa* (made from grinding wheel handles), the *nunchaku* (threshing handles), the *kama* (small, handheld scythes), and the *noburi kama* (a long-handled version of the kama).

All kobudo systems teach interesting techniques and are good as a second or third martial art. Most are considered minor systems, however, because they contain many different skills rather than one dominant type, such as the throwing techniques of judo or the striking found in karate. These characteristics mean that kobudo training often creates students who are "jacks-of-all-trades," rather than masters of one.

Kyudo

In simple terms, *kyudo* is Japanese archery, although in practice it is much more. It is in fact a method of Zen training, full of ritual, and very austere and beautiful. Though not particularly physically demanding, kyudo is one of the hardest martial arts to learn.

Shooting in kyudo involves much more than simply nocking an arrow, aiming, and letting it fly. Everything from the approach to shooting, the tightness with which the bow is held, and the method of aiming (which is not really aiming at all), to the breathing and the state of mind, is choreographed. All the attention to detail is designed to take archers out of themselves and allow them to address the universe without interference from the ego. Though this is a goal shared by all budo forms, nowhere is it as much of a driving force of every motion and ritual as in kyudo.

Because this budo form is less active than most, it is popular with older people and with people who do not like hard exercise. However, the slow movements help develop balance and grace, and do increase physical strength somewhat. The quiet, ritualized practice is an excellent means of improving mental focus, though this should not be confused with relaxation. The first two years or so of kyudo practice are usually frustrating due to the difficulty of learning the basics. It is not an art for those who want to see quick progress or a lot of activity.

Arts of Other Nations

While this book is focused mainly on the Japanese martial arts, many other traditional fighting arts are worthwhile for both physical education and mental discipline. A few carry philosophical roots similar to the Japanese arts. Unfortunately, good instruction in these arts is difficult to find, but so it is with all worthwhile pursuits. For detailed descriptions of these arts and their benefits you will have to seek out books specifically written about them, but some aspects of the most widely available arts are set out below.

China is known for its immense variety of martial arts styles. These arts can be broadly split into two groups: external (those that focus more on muscular development and a higher degree of activity) and internal (those that focus more on efficient use of energy).

Most of the external arts of China can be grouped under the title *kung-fu* ("skill" or "art,")"or *chuan-fa* ("Chinese boxing"), of which there are many substyles, including tiger-crane, monkey, and praying mantis styles. All of these are excellent forms of physical exercise, though their emphasis on circularity makes them more challenging for a beginner than some of the Japanese arts. Their exotic, animal-like movements make them appealing to practice, but they sometimes attract students of less mature character. As always, visit the school before making a commitment, to make sure it has an atmosphere conducive to attaining your goals.

There is also *wu-shu*, which is the modern Chinese term for martial arts, but which usually refers to an acrobatic form of exercise rather than a traditional fighting system. Wu-shu derives from Chinese theater, and most of the "martial arts" seen in Chinese movies would be classified as wu-shu. Jackie Chan, a popular movie start, has an extensive wu-shu background, so one could watch his movies and get a good idea of what wu-shu looks like in action. There are few schools outside of China, however, and this is an art that requires an early start because of the flexibility and energy needed to perform its dynamic moves.

The internal martial arts of China can be loosely divided into three types: *t'ai-chi*, *pa-kua*, and *hsing-i*. Almost everyone has seen t'ai-chi at one time or another. It is a slow, meditative art that is often practiced outdoors by large groups of people. While many older folks practice it solely for physical exercise, t'ai-chi has some very sophisticated fighting applications. A knowledgeable instructor should be able to teach these applications, but a student of t'ai-chi must be patient; it takes a very long time to learn well.

Pa-kua is "eight-trigram" boxing, and has a close relationship with Chinese cosmology. Most of its moves are taught using drills that involve stepping in a circular pattern, with deep stances and turning motions that can be used as blocks, evasions, or throws similar to those found in aikido. Hsing-i is a type of internal boxing that relies on efficient movement and correct alignment of body parts. Most of its techniques involves entering, or stepping inside, an opponent's defensive sphere to execute an attack. It is often practiced by older people, but can be incredibly powerful because of the subtle placement of feet, trunk, and limbs.

Korea offers several interesting martial arts. *Tae-kyon*, an art that focuses almost exclusively on kicking, is considered the mother martial art of several modern systems. It is rarely taught in its pure form today, but one of its descendants, *taekwondo*, may be the most widely practiced martial art on the planet. Taekwondo has the virtue of being very dynamic, since it utilizes many types of kicks and focuses on competition from very early on in the training. It is, in fact, a form of military discipline rather than a martial "art," made a part of Korean military training by a famous general, Choi Hong Hee. It will probably not appeal to those who are less flexible, older, or looking for a deep philosophical component in their martial arts system.

Hapkido is a martial art that uses techniques very similar to those used in aikido. Some historians claim that hapkido was introduced to Korea by the Japanese, and some claim that the Japanese occupation forces borrowed hapkido techniques, which later became aikido. Whatever the case, hapkido is made up of joint locks, throws, and grappling techniques in addition to a liberal variety of kicks and strikes, but it is generally taught with a much more practical self-defense orientation than aikido. It is often taught in connection with taekwondo.

Hwarangdo is probably the Korean martial art with the widest range of techniques, but it is hardly ever taught in its pure form today, having been largely replaced by taekwondo and hapkido. It was probably the closest equivalent to the Japanese feudal arts in terms of having a warrior philosophy, being the art of the Hwarang warriors, who had a centuries-long tradition of fighting the invaders of the Korean peninsula.

Most of the other martial arts that can be studied widely outside of their native countries come from the Indonesian region. Indonesia's native martial art is called *pentjak silat*, and it is really an eclectic mix of skills from a variety of sources. It includes both armed techniques, employing a range of weapons from sticks and knives to whips and sickles, and unarmed techniques, with skills similar to those found in various kung-fu styles, karate, and jujutsu.

The Philippines offer several dynamic martial arts that are highly effective for self-defense. *Kali* is the original martial art of the region. It is a complete system of fighting skills, including armed and unarmed techniques, from which both *escrima* and *arnis*, modern subsystems, are descended. The hallmark of these systems is the fact that the same techniques can be performed with short sticks, knives, or empty hands, with little or no modification. These arts are unique, in fact, in that the armed techniques are usually taught before the empty-hand techniques, an approach opposite to that used by the Japanese.

For those seeking a quick education in self-defense, it would be worthwhile to visit a gym that offers boxing or kickboxing. While these fighting sports do not offer the philosophical dimension of the traditional Asian arts, they do teach good movement skills, are useful for self-defense, and regular practice will get students into great physical condition.

Eight Essential Texts

ALL THOSE INTERESTED in Japanese history, culture, or martial arts should read as much on these subjects as they possibly can. It only makes sense to educate yourself as well as possible in your field of study. There are many good books published about Japanese budo in English, and reading about well-known figures and events in budo history complements and enriches the physical practice.

There are, in fact, five historical figures who are so important in the development of modern Japanese martial arts that anyone who claims to be all proficient in budo must have knowledge of them. Books have been written by or about each of these men. In addition, there have been three pivotal texts written about budo and bushido that are indispensable reading for all martial artists. What follows is a list of these important people and books, with explanations of why they are important. For publication information regarding them, see the annotated bibliography that follows.

Funakoshi Gichin is considered by many to be the father of modern karate. He was one of the men chiefly responsible for bringing karate from Okinawa to Japan in the early part of the twentieth century. The Shotokan school of karate was largely Funakoshi's creation and, like others in this list, he was more than just a martial artist—he was also an educator and an innovator. Every martial artist should read his autobiography, *Karate-Do: My Way of Life*, at least once.

Kano Jigoro was the founder of Kodokan Judo. He synthesized his art from techniques found in early jujutsu systems and sumo. Kano was a great educator, a creative man, and an internationalist. His martial arts system was comprehensive, including a wide range of fighting skills, techniques for improving health, and a theory and philosophy that can be summed up in his motto: *Seiryoku zenyo; jitakyoe* (Efficient use of energy; benefit to self and others). His book, *Kodokan Judo*, is essential reading.

The legend of Miyamoto Musashi is known throughout Japan and the world. He was a seventeenth-century swordsman who fought more than sixty duels and never lost. It is said that he reached a state of enlightenment through his dedication to sword practice. His advice in *The*

Book of Five Rings is so profound that there is always something in it just beyond the understanding of the student. The best martial artists I know will pick up this book once or twice a year to reread it and consider how its meaning relates to them.

Ueshiba Morihei was the founder of aikido. He is considered one of the great philosophers of budo, and regardless of whether you study aikido, exposure to his teachings will help your inner development in the martial arts. We are extremely lucky to have a fine translation of his teachings by John Stevens, called *The Art of Peace: Teachings of the Founder of Aikido*.

That excellent writer John Stevens has also given us another book that makes my list of the best books on budo, *The Sword of No Sword*. *The Sword of No Sword* is about the life and teachings of Yamaoka Tesshu, a Meiji period swordsman, statesman, and perhaps one of the finest calligraphers ever. Tesshu's life exemplified the Zen idea of victory over the self through a robust existence.

The first of the three books that every martial artist must not only read, but totally absorb through years of study, is *Hagakure*, by Yamamoto Tsunetomo. It is a book written by an old samurai lamenting the passing of the time-honored, traditional ways of bushido. Although it contains much that may amuse us today, and some ideas that are simply inappropriate for our era, nowhere else is the spirit of the samurai communicated more clearly or with so much of its essence retained.

The second essential book is *Bushido* by Nitobe Inazo. It is perhaps easier to understand than *Hagakure*, being better organized and having been written expressly for an English-speaking audience, and it communicates concepts found in bushido very well. Because of its intended audience, it lacks something of the heartfelt presentation of Yamamoto's book, but as an introduction to bushido and a periodic refresher, it is superb.

Finally, every martial artist should read Sun Tzu's *The Art of War*. This book spells out, though not always in the clearest terms, how to win battles, individually or in groups. Where Musashi is esoteric, Sun Tzu is methodical, elucidating which factors to consider and how much weight to give them. It may not be clear to beginning martial arts students why this book has value, but once they begin teaching, they will find that *The Art of War* spends many hours off the shelf.

Besides practice, these books offer the best education available in budo. Everyone who claims to be a martial artist should read and reread them and absorb their essence.

Bibliography

THE FOLLOWING BOOKS are ones I recommend to martial arts students. Most are about traditional budo, but a few are about subjects, such as Zen, that are of interest because of their relationship to budo or bushido. This is by no means an exhaustive list, so students should seek out as many other good books as they can find.

Addiss, Steven, and C. Hurst III. *Samurai Painters.* Tokyo: Kodansha, 1983. By showing the brushwork of warriors who were also painters, the authors illuminate several important aspects of their personalities, including their ability to observe, their passion for life, and their strength of character. This is an illuminating complement to the written word for learning about bushido.

Cleary, Thomas. *The Japanese Art of War.* Boston: Shambhala, 1991. A very well-written treatise on the relationship between martial arts, Japanese culture, and Zen. Because this book is written from an academic perspective, it is more useful as a historical overview than a practical guide to martial arts training, but still it is an excellent addition to any martial arts library.

Craig, Darrell. *Iai: The Art of Drawing the Sword*. Boston: Tuttle, 1981. A delightful book on the Mugai style of iaido, illustrated with simple, hand-drawn figures that clearly convey the ideas of the author. Craig explains the basics of Mugai-Ryu, and also offers a liberal dose of samurai culture through stories of old Japan. Even though this work is not very polished, it communicates the spirit of Japanese swordsmanship well.

Davey, H. E. *Living the Japanese Arts and Ways: 45 Paths to Meditation and Beauty*. Berkeley: Stone Bridge, 2003. A unique text among the many books on Japanese cultural arts, this helpful guide identifies the essential concepts shared by many different arts, and gives practical tips on how to identify and practice those concepts. Students of budo, tea ceremony, flower arranging, and any other Japanese personal-enrichment study will find this book extremely helpful.

————. *Unlocking the Secrets of Aiki-Jujutsu*. New York: McGraw Hill, 1997. Davey is that rare Westerner who can both claim a legitimate background in an obscure Japanese martial art and write about it well. He has immersed himself in the cultural arts of Japan, and the advice in this book reflects his depth of knowledge. A great read for those interested in learning about the practical and spiritual aspects of aiki-jujutsu.

Funakoshi, Gichin. *Karate-Do: My Way of Life*. New York: Kodansha, 1975. An autobiography that highlights Funakoshi's martial arts career and his introduction of Okinawan karate to Japan. Easy to read, and written in a clear, entertaining style, the stories and advice found here are inspirational and decidedly informative for students of any martial art.

Herrigel, Eugen. *Zen in the Art of Archery*. New York: Vintage, 1971. This book has had a great influence on the Western understanding of Zen, and rightfully so. Written by a Westerner trying to grasp the secrets of kyudo, Herrigel details his struggles in a way that gives the reader a vivid look at Zen concepts.

Hoffmann, Yoel, ed. *Japanese Death Poems*. Boston: Tuttle, 1986. Zen and Japanese thought taught through one of the most unique products of the bushido culture. There is nothing morbid about these robust poems; they are alive with energy transmitted simply through the words of old warriors and Zen masters.

Hyams, Joe. *Zen in the Martial Arts*. Los Angeles: Tarcher, 1979. Hyams presents anecdotes of his encounters with some of the famous martial arts figures of the early 1970s, including Ed Parker and Bruce Lee. Although few of these stories are actually about Zen, many of them offer good, commonsense advice about various aspects of the martial arts. This is worthwhile reading, especially for novices.

Japanese Travel Bureau. *Martial Arts and Sports in Japan*. Tokyo: JTB, 1993. Meant as a pocket guide for the tourist, this little book actually contains a great deal of accurate information on judo, kendo, sumo, etc. Very helpful for those who are shopping for a first martial art, or those who will visit Japan and want to see budo in its home environment.

Kano, Jigoro. *Kodokan Judo*. New York: Kodansha, 1986. A modern version of Kano's original writings on judo, this is a must read. It describes the evolution of judo from sumo and jujutsu and details the essential skills for beginning, intermediate, and advanced judoists. Serious students of judo will find themselves repeatedly returning to these pages for technical knowledge and inspiration.

Kapp, Leon. *The Craft of the Japanese Sword*. New York: Kodansha, 1987. This visually stunning coffee table book is a must have for those interested in Japanese swords. The author lead his readers through every step of creating a sword as a work of art, including forging, polishing, making fittings, and making scabbards. After reading this fine work, the reader feels as though he has spent a week in a hands-on sword-making class.

Lee, Bruce. *Tao of Jeet Kune Do*. Santa Clara, Calif.: Ohara, 1975. Bruce Lee, famous as a star of martial arts movies, was also an innovator in the real world of fighting arts. Lee's heretical "absorb what is useful" approach is required reading for anyone who wants to understand the impetus for the evolution of modern martial arts, from the classic, traditional forms to the wide-open world of mixed martial arts tournaments.

Lowry, Dave. *Autumn Lightning*. Boston: Shambhala, 1985. The quintessential story of the Westerner who lives with a Japanese martial arts master, learns the art, and finds himself changed by the process. Lowry is a gifted writer who conveys his great knowledge of the Japanese martial arts through entertaining prose that is deceptively easy to read.

Merton, Thomas. *The Way of Chuang Tzu*. Boston: Shambhala, 2004. While not a martial arts text, this is still one of my favorite books about Eastern philosophy. Merton captures the essence of Chuang Tzu with simplicity, insight, and a sense of humor. Well worth reading again and again.

Moeller, Mark. *Karate-do Foundations*. Indianapolis: Masters Press, 1995. In this very useful book on the fundamentals of Shorin-ryu and Shodokan karate, Moeller clearly describes the learning process, history, and philosophy of karate training. Beginners, intermediate students, and teachers will all benefit from the concepts found here.

Morisawa, Jackson. *The Secret of the Target*. New York: Routledge, 1984. An excellent manual of kyudo according to the teachings of the Chozen-ji school of Hawaii, this book treats in depth the relationship between Zen and archery, detailing exactly the movements of the kata and their meanings. A great source of information on kyudo, and very useful for any student of Zen or budo.

Musashi, Miyamoto. *A Book of Five Rings.* Translated by Victor Harris. Woodstock, N.Y.: Overlook, 1974. Probably the most famous book on martial arts and strategy ever published, this book is an effective teacher of strategic concepts in a variety of fields, and has been widely used by businesspeople in building their companies. By offering information that is always slightly beyond the reader's grasp, Musashi lures one into gradually deepening thoughts.

Nicol, C. W. *Moving Zen.* New York: Quill, 1982. A charming history of Nicol's life as a beginning and intermediate karate student. By describing his own difficulties and adventures in learning karate, Nicol illuminates, without lecturing, many of the important aspects of training and Japanese culture.

Nitobe, Inazo. *Bushido: The Soul of Japan.* Boston: Tuttle, 1969. Absolutely the best explanation of bushido in the English language. The author describes the samurai heart of Japan in language that is both well organized and also appealing to the inner senses. Every student of Japanese martial arts must read this book several times.

Reps, Paul, ed. *Zen Flesh, Zen Bones*. Boston: Tuttle, 1957. The most useful Zen book in the English language. Reps has collected Zen stories and other robust writings that actually teach Zen while entertaining the reader. Much more effective and entertaining than any academic treatise on Zen.

Sadler, A. L., trans. *The Code of the Samurai*. Boston: Tuttle, 1992. This is an excellent translation of a sixteenth-century work by Daidoji Yuzan, which advised young samurai on budo and other matters. Though not as pithy as *Hagakure*, this work comes in a close second with its more detailed explanations of certain important concepts, such as right and wrong, bravery, and duty.

Sasamoto, Junzo, and Gordon Warner. *This Is Kendo: The Art of Japanese Fencing*. Boston: Tuttle, 1964. The essential kendo text in English, this work is valuable to every student of the martial arts for its description of the evolution of bushido and swordsmanship, as well as its detailed explanation of the art of kendo.

Sato, Shizuya. *Nihon Jujutsu*. Tokyo: Shoho Insatsu, 1998. Sato is the chief director of Kokusai Budoin, the International Martial Arts Federation, in Japan, and a tenth-degree black belt in Nihon Jujutsu. This book is his handbook for those interested in learning this simple and elegant system of self-defense. It is abundantly illustrated and contains 90 percent of the material Sato teaches to his students at the American Embassy dojo in Tokyo.

Soho, Takuan. *The Unfettered Mind*. Translated by William Scott Wilson. New York: Kodansha, 1986. Takuan, the robust, outspoken Zen master, advised a few of the preeminent swordsmen of the day on how to triumph using Zen. The three remarkable essays in this book convey Zen concepts with authority. Although challenging, this material is nevertheless very important to the serious martial artist.

Stevens, John. *The Art of Peace: Teachings of the Founder of Aikido*. Boston: Shambhala, 1992. Ueshiba Morihei was not only the founder of aikido, but a mystic who put many profound concepts into written and spoken words. For those in search of deep meaning in life, and for those who simply want to understand Ueshiba's far-reaching influence on modern budo, this book is a must-read.

————. *The Sword of No Sword: Life of the Master Warrior Tesshu*. Boston: Shambhala, 1984. One of the most important and inspirational books in the martial arts library. Vital reading for anyone who hopes to learn martial arts as a way of life. Tesshu exemplified the martial ideal of doing everything with total commitment, and reading about his life is an entertaining way to study the history and culture of pre-Meiji Japan.

Suino, Nicklaus. *The Art of Japanese Swordsmanship: A Manual of Eishin-Ryu Iaido*. Boston: Weatherhill, 1994. This book shows the complete set of solo forms in the Eishin school, along with relevant information about the history of swordsmanship, practice methods, and mental aspects of training.

————. *Practice Drills for Japanese Swordsmanship*. Boston: Weatherhill, 1995. A manual of practice drills using the *bokuto* (wooden sword). Trains the student in basic iaido movements: to stand and move with good balance, and to wield the sword with strength.

Sun Tzu. *The Art of War*. Translated by Samuel B. Griffith. London: Oxford, 1963. The quintessential treatise on strategy, very practical and engaging. This is a must-read-annually for martial artists, who should find that every reread yields new insights.

Suzuki, D. T. *Manual of Zen Buddhism*. New York: Grove, 1960. A collection of Zen reading assembled by the grandfather of Zen in the West, this book contains sutras, koans, and stories meant to assist Zen monks in their studies. From simple and amusing to extremely abstruse, the writings here teach rather than describe the Zen state of mind.

Takagi, Takeshi. *A Comparison of Bushido and Chivalry*. Translated by Matsuno Tsuneyoshi. Osaka, Japan: TM International Academy, 1984. A good source of stories about samurai warriors and lists of warrior virtues, this book is written in awkward nonnative English but contains much vital information on budo and bushido.

Tohei, Koichi. *Ki in Daily Life*. New York: Kodansha. Tohei's deep understanding of *ki*, or *chi* (intrinsic energy), permeates this book, which is an excellent introduction for those interested in aikido, chi gong, t'ai-chi, or those simply interested in improving their own lives through an understanding of the life force. Tohei is a seminal figure in the migration of Asian arts to North America, and the writing in his book is both forceful and clear.

Warner, Gordon, and Donn Draeger. *Japanese Swordsmanship*. New York: Weatherhill, 1986. One of the first and finest books written on iaido in English, by two of the first experts in the field. The book has an extensive historical section, written in Draeger's inimitable style, and a detailed section on the fundamentals of *seitei iai*. A good educational text for any student of swordsmanship, though probably best for those who are students of the techniques shown.

Watson, Lyall. *Sumo*. London: Sidgewick & Jackson, 1988. A richly illustrated guide to the most essentially Japanese of martial sports. Describes techniques and sumo culture, and lists many of the top *rikishi* (sumo players) of the time when the book was written. Useful for sumo fans and for judoists, who can study the relationship between sumo skills and those used in judo.

Yamamoto, Kansuke. *Heiho Okugisho: The Secret of High Strategy*. Translated by Toshishiro Obata. Hollywood, Calif.:

W. M. Hawley, 1994. A reprinting with translations of writings on strategy in swordsmanship, this collection was first begun in 1571 and modified several times through the years. This book is full of practical advice for the samurai swordfighter, and the writings and pictures are evocative of a bygone era.

Yamamoto, Tsunetomo. *Hagakure: The Book of the Samurai*. Translated by William Scott Wilson. New York: Kodansha, 1979. An indispensable book for any serious student of Japanese martial arts or culture. Expresses, rather than describes, bushido and the samurai culture, and does so in an inspiring way that makes it one of the most important books in any martial artist's library.

Resources

THERE ARE MANY martial arts organizations, but very few that advocate real Japanese budo. Even among those that do promote traditional budo, the quality varies tremendously, so I have listed only the few that I can vouch for through personal contact. There may be other worthwhile organizations, but be sure to get as much information about an organization as you can before making any commitment.

Aikikai Foundation
17-18 Wakamatsu-Cho
Shinjuku-Ku
Tokyo, Japan 162-0056
Phone: 81-03-3203-9236
www.aikikai.or.jp

The Aikikai was established in 1940 by the founder of aikido, Morihei Ueshiba, to preserve and promote the true ideals of aikido. After Ueshiba died in 1969, his son Kisshomaru Ueshiba took over, and the organization is presently run by Moriteru Ueshiba, his grandson.

Art of Japanese Swordsmanship (AJS) and
   North American Iaido Association (NAIA)
P.O. Box 221
Traverse City, MI 49685-0221
Phone: 231-649-6485
www.artofjapaneseswordsmanship.com
info@artofjapaneseswordsmanship.com

AJS and NAIA are the organizations run by Nicklaus Suino to promote and popularize the art of Japanese swordsmanship. They do not grant rank, but provide opportunities for training in seminars, classes, and private lessons, and also promote demonstrations and forms tournaments in iaido.

International Martial Arts Federation (IMAF)
3-24-1 Higashiyamato-Shi
Tokyo, Japan 207-0012
Phone: 81-42-565-9146
www.imaf.com

A prestigious organization that grants ranks from its headquarters in Tokyo, IMAF was founded by some of the most famous historical figures in Japanese budo, including Mifune Kyuzo, Ito Kazuo, Sato Shizuya, Nakayama Hakudo, and Otsuka Hironori. IMAF is one of a few Japanese organizations sanctioned by the Imperial family, allowing it to grant titles (*renshi, kyoshi, hanshi*) as well as belt ranks.

Kodokan
1-16-030 Kasuga
Bunkyo-Ku
Tokyo, Japan 112-0003
Phone: 81-03-3818-4172
www.kodokan.org

This is the original judo organization, founded by Kano Jigoro, involved today in the worldwide promotion of sport judo. The Kodokan has a large facility in Tokyo that includes several dojos, a library, and research offices.

Shudokan Martial Arts Association (SMAA)
73 South Street
Granby, MA 01033
Phone: 413-467-2423
www.michionline.org/smaa

Founded by Walter E. Todd, who held the rank of kyoshi, 8th dan in judo, 8th dan in karate-do, and 6th dan in aikido. Todd studied with such famous figures as Mifune Kyuzo, Tomiki Kenji, and Toyama Kanken. The SMAA is now run by reputable leaders in North American martial arts.

Yoshinkan Aikido Federation
The International Yoshinkai Aikido Federation
Aikido Yoshinkan Hombu Dojo
3F Takayama Building
28-8, 2-Chome
Kami-Ochiai
Shinjuku-Ku
Tokyo, Japan 161
www.yoshinkan-aikido.org

Headquarters of Yoshinkai Aikido, a branch of Ueshiba Morihei's martial art, which was developed by the late Shioda Gozo. The Yoshinkan holds classes for all levels, runs a police training program, and helps to promote aikido around the world.